Justifiable Tone

Justifiable Tone

T. Lynne Comparato

Thunderbird Press

Justifiable Tone
Copyright ©2018 by T. Lynne Comparato

Published by Thunderbird Press
P.O. Box 524, Rancho Mirage, California 92270
thunderbirdpress@dc.rr.com

Book design by Jean Denning
Cover design by Karoline Kessler

Library of Congress Control Number: 2018956442

Comparato, T. Lynne
Justifiable Tone

ISBN: 978-1725679429

Printed in the United States of America

*To the memory of my extraordinary
daughter, and her indomitable spirit.
"You are Always In My Heart"*

Acknowledgments

THANK YOU ...

I would like to extend my heartfelt gratitude to:

Leonard Cohen ... for shining the light all these years. I miss you!

Sol Feigman ... for believing in me from day one.

Gail Higgins ... for your unwavering patience and guidance as I sorted it all out.

Audrey Cerniglia ... for your unstoppable and relentless optimism and encouragement on this project.

Vinny Stoppia ... for pointing me in the right direction, and then giving me a much needed push forward.

Karoline Kessler ... for your outstanding graphics input on the front and back covers, and the conversion of this manuscript to InDesign.

A special thanks to Jean Denning ... who brought this project to life with charm and elegance.

Introduction

Mom and I shopped at the A&P on 103rd Street on Fridays in the early evening. We had a hand cart to carry the groceries home. Sometimes the cart was so heavy that we had to hold it, both of us together; and when we got home, we had to maneuver the cart up two flights of stairs in order to reach our third-floor apartment. This was something that we always did together.

Once in a while, on weekdays Mom would give me money with instructions to go and buy some Sicilian pizza on 104th Street, and she would meet my brother and me at home for lunch.

Mom loved her desserts. Charlotte Russe was one of her favorites. She dived into them, and her eyes would light up. It was fun watching her eat dessert.

I remember my childhood being filled with emotional pain and humiliation, but the Friday-night excursions and the lunches of Sicilian pizza are good memories.

My parents never considered the gravity of the responsibility that resulted in the decision to have children. It never occurred to them that in addition to food and clothing, guidance and nurturing were required. Unfortunately, I paid for their shortcomings with a cold and barren childhood. My lack of confidence and longing for recognition made my school days awkward and difficult.

During my young childhood, and even part of my early teen years, it wasn't that my values were misdirected, as much as I had no values. I had no awareness of well-being. Under these limited conditions, I did amazingly well in surviving to young adulthood … where I then plunged deeply into the darkest and most destructive period of my life. I look back at this period of time as true hell.

Not knowing myself at all, except for rare glimpses of who I thought I could be—and attempting to escape from an empty and sad childhood that never yielded as much as a sincere smile—at a very young age I married a shallow, weak and selfish man. Through that I learned another entire dimension of reckless self destruction—a dimension of emotional torture and humiliation so intense that I lived each day in a world of disappointment, self loathing and shame. I hated my life. Looking back now, I am still amazed that I was able to climb out of that black hole and become the person that I am today.

In life, you cannot find a remedy until you recognize the problem … until you put words to it and face it head on … and until you are willing to claw your way back, and begin again in the direction of the light and truth that only your own soul knows.

I am forever grateful for the courage to begin the journey back that would carry me to a world of self discovery and deep core beliefs.

The relief of distancing myself from the person I married produced a great joy, lifting me to a place filled with pride and self-respect that I never dreamed possible.

I was young, barely twenty-three, and for the first time in my life, I was clear. Seeing myself, and best of all, liking what I saw gave me a new understanding of life. My journey was just beginning, and I would do the work and always remain true to myself. I was really alive, and in the state of grace.

Contents

Continued ...

1

Beginnings

I have to be honest. Neither of my parents drank, or shouted at each other, nor did they scream at me. They both worked. They paid the bills. They put food on the table.

My mother attempted to cook, and dinner was mostly bland, dry and often burnt. The point is, however, that she bought the food and cooked it.

Mom's housekeeping skills were quite underdeveloped. Our home was always very messy, and that is understated. Our three-bedroom apartment was figuratively like living in a pig pen. Our bathroom was rarely cleaned. The towel that hung on the bar (unless it had fallen to the floor), was almost never changed. We never had napkins in the house, so when we sat down to dinner, the kitchen towel was passed around as needed, and then would continue on to dry dishes or wet hands. Kitchen towels would go for days before being changed. This all seemed quite normal to me.

My room, however, was immaculate. Everything was in its proper place. Clothes were folded, dresser dusted, bed made. So one might walk through the apartment climbing over piles of out-of-place clutter from room to room, then open my door and behold a meticulous museum like view of an eight-year-old's room. This was the only space that I could control and reflected the order and respect that I longed for in my life.

My brother was not quite two years older than I. My mother adored him. She doted on him, and catered to his every whim. Howard was then, and remained, the most important thing in my mother's life. If Mom could have followed a thought to its natural conclusion (which was doubtful), it would have stated clearly that if you were alive, and you didn't have a penis, you were merely an afterthought with very little consequence. I was the younger female child who was mostly in her way.

My brother was great looking. He was smart and talented; but unfortunately, he never got past handsome. He spent a great deal of time looking in the mirror and combing his hair, never applying himself to a single productive task. Howard used his brains mainly to figure out ways to indulge his desires without working for them; and he learned from an early age how to lie, cheat, and steal, while remaining in people's good graces. He knew how to use people for his own gain, and through his entire life, never accomplished anything.

My brother was horribly disrespectful to my mother, and my childhood was filled with screaming matches between the two.

But oh how mom loved him!

And she delivered a strong message to him … that looks were most important. Nothing pleased Mom more than seeing the girls chase him.

As time marched on, Howard just went along combing his hair, and abusing anyone who got in his way, including and foremost … me. I never got in his way, but the close proximity of our space growing up together made me a convenient target for his tyranny.

My dad divorced my mother when I was around the age of six. He met and fell madly in love with a successful, spirited, ambitious woman named Margaret. In those days, divorce was much less trendy than now.

This all would have been okay, if there had been any semblance of order and normalcy. But my mother just couldn't accept the reality of what was happening. So with a wink and a nod, she invited my dad to visit often. The agreement that they came to was: not to reveal to Mom's friends and family (this included my brother and me), that they were divorced. Dad would drop by two or three times a week for afternoon visits that would once in a while include dinner. If anyone asked why my father's presence at home was so limited, my mother simply said that he worked two or three jobs, and had to sleep there sometimes. She held her head up and kept her pride intact, while living a charade. My father's wife, Margaret, never caught on, and life went on for years that way.

So I grew up thinking that my father worked three jobs, while my mother became my father's mistress, and my brother became proficient at playing hooky and stealing cars. My mother traded dignity for financial security and revenge.

By the time I reached the age of thirteen, we had moved from the city to the suburbs. When I say we, I mean my mother, my brother, me, and my pretend father, who still showed up once or twice a week.

I was a good student, and was about to embark on a new educational experience … high school. I went through all the motions, but nothing in my life seemed real to me. I was still a blank slate. There was no self awareness, and no sense of sad or glad. There was no feeling of okayness. Life to me was a straight line.

My mother and brother continued to fight. I couldn't stand the drama, and vowed to myself that I would never allow this type of upheaval to exist in my life, no matter where I wound up. My mother was ill tempered and often out of sorts. I began to recognize some negative traits in her behavior that were directly connected to her relationship with me, and I felt used by her, emotionally. She was often abusive, disrespectful, and derisive towards me.

Maybe she had been that way all along, but it was becoming increasingly clear. She was difficult to be around, and I was asserting more and more independence. This was infuriating to her. In her life, I was the only thing that she had control of. She certainly never controlled my brother. Her marriage was make believe, and now she was losing control over me—the one person in her life who in fact loved her. Now I could not deny what I was actually seeing. I began to dislike her. She started to appear small to me. This was the very beginning of my insight into my mother as a person. It is significant because it was also an introduction to my own self awareness, and understanding of honesty and integrity.

No one had ever taught me about the morality of right and wrong … about kindness and compassion, and how gravely important it is to hear one's own truth, and then trust it and live it.

This was an emotional genesis for me. I would lose sight of it for a while, but these beliefs were planted firmly in my soul, and they would find me again. And they would save my life.

2

Howard

In my entire life, I have never seen any person that could rival the obvious disregard for people that my brother, Howard, had for everyone, whether it was a casual acquaintance or a family member, and there was nothing sneaky about his behavior. Howard's quest in life was pleasing Howard — nothing more, nothing less. Anyone or anything that got in his way was trampled, and kicked aside without a second thought. He never developed his huge and notable capacity for logic and intelligence. His downhill slide on the road to corruption began as a young teenager, and picked up speed throughout his life.

Having lived with these abnormal circumstances my whole life, I learned how to desensitize myself from emotional trauma. I was always shocked at Howard's lighthearted jump from one mischievous endeavor to another. And I can remember vividly a fixed emotional state of disbelief that I would find myself in, time after time. I knew how to bury anxiety and stress so that I could proceed day to day in my own life. Once in a while the shock of the daily reality of Howard's flagrant disrespect for any authority, or civilized rule, would surface in my mind. I was so disturbed by it that I would actually feel a physical flush throughout my body. I did my best to make these moments of truth as short and bearable as possible, so that I could slip back into denial and continue on in my own life.

At the age of thirteen, Howard took my mother's car keys and had a key made for himself. He would, on a regular basis, ditch school, walk about fifteen blocks to where my mother worked, take the car, joyride all day, and then return the car to its parking spot before my mother's quitting time. This went on for weeks. Once in a while when Howard was returning the car at the end of the day, he found that the original parking space was filled, and he had to re-park the car in a different spot.

There were many nights that my mother would casually remark how strange it was, that after work, she would find her car down the block from where she had parked it earlier. After eight or ten of these instances, she finally caught on. This led to no more than a quick reprimand, and that episode was put to bed. Mom changed the ignition and had new keys made, but Howard simply replicated the new key, and would regularly sneak out his window at night and joy ride for hours. Getting caught did not faze my brother in the least. Not long after that, Howard began stealing cars in earnest. The police would bring him home often.

My father was never told about the action-packed criminal life of his thirteen-year-old son until there were so many serious offenses that he would have to be told. Dad, like myself, was in a state of disbelief, which at least validated my own shock and disbelief. The difference was that where my disbelief turned to fear and confusion, Dad's disbelief turned to anger. So after much turmoil, and frustration, it was decided to send Howard off to military school.

As my brother prepared for this new chapter in his life, all the attention of our twisted little household was focused on the exorbitant amount of money that was required just to get him in the door of this well-reputed school. His uniforms alone would cost a staggering amount of money. Tuition to this prestigious school was so far out of our reach that it meant my mother and I would have to drastically change our eating habits. We ate fewer meals, and they consisted mostly of pasta and a vegetable.

To me, there would finally be peace in the house. To Mom, her pride and joy was now going to a distinguished military academy. She could not get enough of the sight of him, her wonderful and handsome boy, in uniform. This was an orgasmic moment for good ole Mom.

So off he went in all his glory. Glory was the one thing that Howard had down. And it was at this time that I noticed a new development in his demeanor. It was "a swagger." From that time on, my brother never walked … he strutted!

Two or three months after my brother began his new life, I was home for lunch one day when the phone rang. I, being home alone, answered it. It was Howard's school. Instead of asking to have one of my parents call them back, or instead of calling back at a later time when my parents might be home, the person on the other end of the phone reported to me (a twelve-year old), that Howard had run away from school. He and another boy broke into a vacation house somewhere in the country and got caught. They were in jail. And, by the way, he said Howard was to be expelled!

I was beyond upset or disturbed. I became nauseous. I despised my brother!

And that is how our move to the suburbs came to be. We would now get away from the crowded city, and go where there were no juvenile delinquents around to corrupt Howard.

3

Calm Before the Storm

I was an "A" student, with good friends, and was accepted into an excellent parochial high school. I can't say that I was actually enjoying my life, but I was living it. At this point, I had learned on my own, the difference between right and wrong, and the value of friends. I was a little sad to leave the city, but we were moving into a house with a yard where there was clean fresh air. Relocating meant that I would be attending public school for the first time, and I was up for it.

Howard and Mom were still screaming at each other. Dad was still dutifully keeping his scheduled visits. We were all still living the fantasy of a normal family, with undivorced parents, behind a white picket fence. And it happens that we did have a white picket fence around our house.

School for me was okay. I had made good friends. I was part of a chorale group and participated in many plays, concerts, and other activities. I was learning the value of self-respect. I had gained a little confidence, and was tolerating my strange family life.

The summer of my fifteenth year, I got a job and worked afternoons, early evenings, and weekends, waitressing and car hopping at a local fast food place. During the holiday season, I worked the gift shop at Gertz department store. I was a good responsible worker. I made some money, and so I guess you might say that I was almost a normal teenager.

Howard had predictably quit school, and was working for a roofing company. He worked on all the days that he could drag himself out of bed in the mornings. That job, of course, did not last long. His life had so many twists and turns that I can't remember all the incidental disasters ... just the major ones. The major ones were complete upheavals. They were disturbances that rocked the entire make-believe life that we all had settled into.

Before Howard had attained his senior driver's license, he hired a woman to go into a bank with my mother's savings account passbook. He instructed her to withdraw a large sum of money. He then put a hefty down payment on a brand new shiny black Ford Thunderbird. He was not yet old enough for a senior license. He had quit school, and didn't have a job. But he pulled that off!

On the very afternoon that he took ownership of this beautiful car, he was driving on the main thoroughfare by our house at the exact moment that my father was arriving home for his conjugal visit. Dad stopped for a red light, and turned his head to the left. There, right next to him, in all his splendor and glory, was Howard, who was stopped for the same red light in his beautiful brand new Thunderbird.

Was Dad aghast? Well I don't think aghast covers it!

At this point in time I was experiencing my first love. I had enjoyed the company of other boyfriends, and the pleasures of a kiss before. But this! This was the most pleasurable and sweet experience of my life to date. He was a big strapping boy, with confidence and charisma. Tom was the nephew of a childhood friend of my mother's. We met at a graduation party. He and I went to Forest Park, and hand in hand, we walked and talked for hours. After a couple of calls and dates, we fell madly in love. His parents were wonderful, and welcomed me into their home whenever I was in town. Tom was the second of three brothers. They were a functioning family that lived in a quiet home where there was love, caring, trust and respect. It was wonderful to love someone, and so nice to be welcomed by his family.

When I was with him, I felt happy and normal. This was my first strong physical attraction. I loved the make-out sessions, and Tom and I would proudly walk around with hickeys displayed on the side of our necks.

Tom lived close to my old neighborhood in the city, so distance prevented us from being together as much as we would have liked. The Long Island Railroad became a major player in our relationship. I was always saddened hearing the sound of the train chugging and the whistle blowing after dark, because it told me that the train was taking him away from me. To this day, I think of Tom whenever I hear the sound of a train whistle. Tom wrote me wonderful letters, many of them. And I treasured each one.

My mother was becoming more and more irritating as each day passed. She had a negative opinion about everything. She was whiny and mean spirited. It was just the two of us now, Mom and me.

Howard's girlfriend had become pregnant, and he got married and moved to a small three-room apartment a couple of towns over. For the short time that they were in that apartment, I got caught up in the fairy tale element. All I saw was this cute little home, with this cute little family. And I wanted that, too. If only I could marry Tom and have a cute little place to live, just like that!

My wonderful first love eventually played itself out, and left me broken hearted. Mom never liked Tom. She resented him from the beginning. She found ways to humiliate and embarrass me in front of him. I felt like my mother's hooks were embedded deep inside of me, and that because I was her child, she intended to dictate my every thought and action. When Tom and I broke up, the more I missed him, the more I hated my mother.

To the contrary, I grew fond of my father over the years. I'm not sure why — maybe because he was so sure of himself, or maybe because he looked at me with a hint of pride. Dad and I could communicate on the same level, and aside from the parent-child thing, we liked each other. Dad could not relate to Howard. Howard was some out-of-control entity that my mother had created. She built him brick by brick.

I can vividly remember Mom buying Howard a pair of Florsheim shoes when he was in the fourth grade. Shoes in those days were three or four dollars. A pair of Florsheims was thirty dollars. I can still see the look on Dad's face, and hear the incredulous tone in his voice, when he became aware of Howard's Florsheim shoes. He said, "I'm forty years old, and I still don't own a pair of Florsheim Shoes!"

But Howard was Mom's crowning achievement, her very own penis child! In my mother's book, most accomplishments, desires, activities, expressions or ambitions were appropriate only if you were a boy. "Girls can't do that," was a statement that I heard repeatedly in my life. And if a girl dared to compete with, and/or excel at an activity that Mom deemed appropriate for boys only ... well, that might be considered cause for shame.

By the way, once I found myself, I excelled at everything I dared to try.

"*Shame*" ... what a word! Adults who use that word with children may just as well rape them. The word is a useless, destructive travesty, and it is used as a power play. Once children hear that word in reference to themselves, the damage is done. And it is irreversible. "*Shame*" should be banished from the English language.

In and out of Howard's antics dealing with my mother's foul nonsensical mood swings, acknowledging my father's entrances and exits as he came and went ... I continued to work. I bought myself contact lenses. I obtained my junior driver's license, and demanded the use of the car (because after all, Howard was driving it when he was twelve). And I must say that Mom was pretty good about that.

So I had wheels when I needed them. I had money in my pocket, I was doing okay in school. I was tolerating my weird home life. I was feeling a little cocky, but not in an obnoxious way. I was almost on an upswing!

If only I had stayed the course.

4

The Long, Slow Journey Into Hell

I have no answers, even to myself, about how or why I drifted so far into darkness. I'm sure that a large part of the decisions I made and options that I chose were related to the disrespect that I felt for my mother, and certainly the obvious lack of respect and courtesy that she directed toward me.

There were good things about me, about my character, things I liked about myself, that were entirely unrecognized by my parents. The value I saw in myself that made me special was completely obscured at home. Even at a very young age, I was able to appreciate virtue. And there was no virtue in my family. They were all wrapped up in themselves, and couldn't get past their own immediate shallow needs. I was not comfortable there. But I did not have a tangible understanding of how or why I felt this way. Something in that house was just wrong.

It was around this time that my parents decided to *"come clean."*

Since my father was rarely home, I had assumed that he was actively pursuing other women. But I never dreamed ... never in a million years ... that they had been divorced for over a decade!

Was I flabbergasted? Was I outraged? I was numb!

That two people could live in a world of lies ... that my mother would allow herself to be stripped completely of all dignity, and self create a life of degradation ... that my father could marry another woman, and allow that woman to think she was participating in a real relationship when in reality, she was just an unsuspecting player in this sick convoluted lie. A lie that provided Dad with two lives. A lie that would feed my mother's pressing, crucial need with the path to denial that she had indeed lost her husband to another woman, while also providing Mom with an easy convenient avenue to satisfy her ongoing and never-ending obsession for revenge.

So not only did these two people, "these two small people," live a life of fiction and deceit, these two selfish fucks created a life of bogus, pretentious lies for their children to grow up in. Children who, in addition to living in this sham, were denied even the smallest consideration for basic dignity.

And now ... they are both telling me their story, their own side of it, and with not a trace of tenderness ... and certainly no apologies.

Was I numb? I was dead!

To make matters more confusing after the "big reveal," the next thing on the agenda that day was: "So what should we do about supper?"

I think it would be safe to assume that it was at this juncture that I began my swift decline. While waitressing, I had noticed a man who came in each afternoon around five o'clock. He always sat on the end stool at the counter, facing the kitchen. He always ordered the same thing: a deluxe hamburger platter, onion rings and a coke.

He wasn't bad looking, but definitely not my type ... but that could be overlooked! His left ear stuck out a bit ... but that could be overlooked! He reminded me a bit of a "hick." I had only heard that word a couple of times, but this guy reminded me of what that word probably meant. His clothes didn't fit him exactly right. His pant legs and shirt sleeves were a little too short ... but that could be overlooked! Let's see, is there something, anything about this guy that doesn't have to be overlooked?

We began talking each day, and after a while started to date. He seemed intelligent, but his voice intonations and expressions reminded me of the Beverly Hillbillies. He was new to the area. He had come up north from Florida, where the police were looking for him because he had beaten up his ex-wife's father.

Yes, that's right, it could all be overlooked! After all, I had been living in a nightmare that seemed perfectly normal to my parents. This guy was twenty-three, and working. He could probably swing a cute little three-room apartment, like the one my brother used to have.

I did not love him. I did not find him attractive. He was weak willed, with no self discipline. He did not make a lot of money. I mean, if you looked hard enough, I guess you could say that he was sort of a nice guy; that is, if you looked hard.

So a couple of months later, I made the announcement to my mother that I would be quitting school (after all, Howard did), and marrying Brian.

Let me stress at this point, that I was *not* pregnant!

I was giving up my entire academic future, and marrying this deficient human being simply because I felt like it. "And what do you think about that, Mom and Dad?"

My mother's lack of common sense and conviction never ceased to amaze me. She began to rattle on about wedding invitations and receptions and dresses. Once again I was aghast! All I could do was stare at her, astonished that she would readily accept and allow her sixteen-year-old honor student to quit school and marry a barely acceptable looking, barely educated hick, who was wanted by the law in Florida. I was tossing my life in the toilet, and she was flushing.

Dad was a different story. He was stunned at this new development in my life. He was outraged and angered. Even though he had never given me the time of day, nor taken even one moment of his time to really connect with me, somewhere in the far corner of his heart, he sort of liked me. I was the one shot he had at being the proud father of a doctor or a lawyer. And now suddenly at the age of sixteen, I was ending my life as I knew it. It didn't make any sense to him. It didn't make any sense to me either, but I was most definitely doing it. And this would leave him, the only one of my parents who actually had a functioning thinking process ... to face the reality that he was a complete failure as a father.

I knew exactly how both my parents would react to Brian, and I was right on target. My mother, whom I came to regularly regard as mindless, smiled and flirted with Brian. My father looked at him with an expression of disbelief. Dad looked at him; then he looked at me. The intensity of his expression spoke volumes. Dad picked up on the short sleeves immediately. After Brian left, Dad eluded to the fact that if I didn't come back to reality quickly, Dad was going to break my legs.

"Doesn't he have any clothes that fit him?" he shouted. "You're going to marry a goddamned hick?" he shouted again.

He continued ranting and raving along those lines, while Mom was busy hoping that her plans for the wedding invitations would not be spoiled.

Dad had to be careful, because don't forget he had a colossal secret. A whole other life, and the other life contained a wife who had no idea that he, for the past ten years was visiting us twice a week. He had no children with Margaret, and except for his excursions to our house, Dad and Margaret had a grand marriage. They had a business together and owned an apartment in the city. Margaret assumed that except for sending child support, there had been no contact at all.

So essentially, any new family member on this end would sort of have to be "read in." They would have to be briefed. Before they were briefed, they would have to somehow show that they were worthy of trust.

I would guess that Brian and his ill-fitting clothes put the fear of God into Dad, for the moment anyway.

I felt sorry for Margaret. It was as if she was the brunt of a cruel joke. We all knew the dirty little details now, except for her. She looked like such a fool. How could Dad do this to her? And of course, this was all carefully orchestrated by my mother, because if she couldn't have Dad, then no one could. Mom would fix Margaret's wagon, and she didn't care who got hurt in the process.

After the truth came out on this end, I suggested that I might meet Margaret. But that was out of the question, because Dad had woven so intricate a web of lies that it would have been nearly impossible not to get tripped up, exposing Dad's dirty little game.

I think at the very beginning, Dad wanted Howard and me to know Margaret. But Mom would not even consider it. Dad now took to telling me what a beautiful, spirited, sexy, woman Margaret was. It was "Margaret this" and "Margaret that" … while he parked himself in my mother's house twice a week.

I felt like I was becoming more and more distorted emotionally. I was losing sight of any preconceived idea that I might have developed, about how life was supposed to be. So Brian and I announced that we would move our wedding date up. Instead of the planned formal September wedding, we would have a small ceremony in August.

I was *not* looking forward to this, and I still can't believe that I got married to Brian at the age of sixteen. But I was confused and wounded by the years of lies and neglect at home. And now, with the cold hard facts exposed, I was angry. I told myself that for better or worse, I would honor my commitment to this marriage. I would be a good wife, and I would stick with it. The night before the ceremony, we went to Coney Island and rode the cyclone. The following afternoon, I took the deepest plunge of my young life. Brian wore his infamous suit with his wrists sticking out. When the ceremony was over, he turned to me and said, "Well, we're hitched!"

At that moment, an intuitive foreboding premonition swept through me. I wished that I could go home with my friends who had stood up for us at our ceremony.

Did I do this just to get a rise out of my father?

Brian and I went to Tad's Steak House for dinner, and then we were off to Niagara Falls in our tiny little sports car.

I lay in bed that night missing my friends and the familiarity of my home. I lay there asking myself, "What in the world did I do?" And I reiterated my promise to myself that I would honor my commitment to this marriage.

What I remember most about the honeymoon was that the song "Danke Schoen" by Wayne Newton was playing every time we turned on the radio. It was playing in every restaurant and café we went into day after day, and for some reason it always made me sad. It was on my honeymoon that I first got a glimpse of what was to come in this marriage. I was seeing a side of Brian that I had never seen before. I did not feel loved, or secure. I kept telling myself not to second guess, but go forward.

Shortly after we were married, Mom decided that she wanted boyfriends in her life. And Dad spent most of his time with Margaret. Brian and I were able to buy a house with no down payment. It was a small house with four small bedrooms. We bought it from a middle-aged Chinese couple named Mr. and Mrs. Quanck. It was located in the far reaches of the South Shore, a good hour away from my mother, and maybe two hours from where my father lived.

My mother would stop by with a boyfriend once in a while, and act ridiculous.

But oddly, my dad called me often and drove out to see me several times. He would come during the day when I was alone. We sat at the table for hours, and he would talk to me about his life. He talked — about the pride he felt becoming a Marine, and serving his country; about how very much he cherished his mother (my grandmother). He took notice of how meticulously I kept the house.

My relationship with my father developed during this time period. On one occasion, he drove out, picked me up, and took me all the way back into the city, where we spent the day at the racetrack. He showed me how he picked horses, and how to bet on them. We watched a couple of races, got a hot dog, and then he drove me back home. Dad had no patience for long drives, or traffic, so this excursion was particularly impressive.

My impression of this late-blooming, parent-child relationship was that he was seeing me for the first time, and that he realized his thoughtless behavior over the years may well have caused this monumental upheaval in my life. He was sincere and tender, and he did his best to accept the resulting circumstances.

My capacity to feel was so underdeveloped that I could not fully appreciate Dad's sudden display of affection. But, I did recognize his sincere effort. And even now, as I write this, I am so grateful for those few memories of the time that we spent together. Unfortunately, it was short lived.

I never in all of my life spent even a single moment with my mother that was real. Mom and I never, ever connected. Not once! My mother's craving for attention and praise was unquenchable. It was a flagrant immature display. Mom saw people and events only in terms of how they affected her. She was narrow minded to such an extent that being in her company was a burden. Even if she was sitting quietly, her presence was offensive. As time passed, her immature behavior became more and more exaggerated. I was extremely embarrassed by her.

I completely understood my parents' divorce. What I didn't understand was the relationship that followed. Dad was a fuck; there was no doubt about it. He had positioned himself in the center of many lives, and chose, as he pleased, which role he desired to play on any given day. But Dad was aware of himself and of the games that he played. He owned who he was, bad or good. He enjoyed the challenge of running back and forth, switching from role to role, and the excitement of almost, but not quite, getting caught. I'm certainly not pinning any medals on him. And I am aware that his antics took a huge toll on me … but I liked Dad. He was a real character. He made no apologies to anyone ever. And my guess is that given the chance, he might do it all over again, without changing a thing.

Mom was incompetent. She was an ignorant person who was mean spirited and scathing. Oddly, even though she had never accomplished anything or made an effort to get the blood flowing in her brain—and even though she seemed incapable of completing a thought—Mom was arrogant. She criticized and ridiculed everyone. Spending time with her would readily cause me to question my ability to think.

5

Turning up the Heat

The complexity of my confusion grew. Brian and I were so incompatible, as you might guess.

I had no experience in maintaining financial stability. Brian was completely irresponsible with money, so bills never got paid. We took advantage of every come-on add that we saw in magazines. I assumed that he knew what he was doing. We used credit as if it was a gift from God. We went through car after car. We just drove cars until they stopped; then we looked for another.

Sex meant nothing to me. There was no love making in this marriage ... no joining of spirits ... no soul touching ... just a repetitive movement. I was criticized if I liked it, and scolded if I didn't. My natural capacity for passion was simply squelched. So I came to regard sex as a chore, not my favorite chore either, a chore that I was obligated to perform. And I did my duty, making every effort to have the correct attitude. After a while, I could not stand Brian coming near me.

We only stayed in that first house for a short time, a few months maybe. I missed my friends. We were so far away from everyone, so we decided to move back. Even though we owned that house, we didn't sell it. We didn't know how to sell a house, and we didn't feel like learning. So we just left. We moved out and just left the house there to fend for itself. A few weeks later, the real estate agent who sold us the place found us and asked about our sad, abandoned little house. We simply said, "Oh, we don't want it anymore. You can have it!"

I wish I were making this up.

Our next episode landed us close to our old familiar neighborhood. We somehow managed to get ourselves into a lovely three-room apartment in a large complex. I loved it! We bought living room furniture, curtains and drapes on a W.T. Grants department store credit card. The apartment was perfect. We were comfortable there. The place was a financial stretch, but it was doable. If we got into a jam with money, we simply sold stuff—like jewelry (including my engagement ring) and my piano. The marriage was nearing seven or eight months old now, as we settled into a quiet period in our apartment.

During our honeymoon, I had seen a glimpse of a real ugly side of Brian's temperament. It seemed like there was a potential for some serious rage. In all of my tumultuous life before marriage, I did not have any experience with actual full-blown rage. And it would be an understatement if I said that it gave me a strong sense of pause. There was an incident in our house on the south shore when, with no warning signs, literally none, I had no idea that Brian was even agitated when he threw a six-quart pot of soaking beans across the room and walked out of the house. I had never seen anything like this. I stood there dumbfounded, thinking *wow, I guess he was angry*. We did get past that, but the tantrum was sobering, and it stayed with me. After a few weeks, I told myself that it was just something that happened, and in all probability, would never happen again.

So now here we are in our great little apartment, and I could hardly contain my enthusiasm, because we were going to hang drapes in our bedroom. The drapes were wall to wall and exceptionally heavy, so the rods had to be substantially secured into the wall. They were almost up, and looked great, but the right side did not want to click in all the way. Brian was kneeling on the dresser, trying to work it. I guess he was losing his patience because suddenly and without warning, he ripped the rod with the drapes attached, right out of the wall, taking part of the wall with them. He slammed everything on the floor, and simply said, "There ... now let's go to bed!" Aside from the disappointment over the drapes that I had been looking forward to, aside from that ... I stood dumbfounded once again, and took a long hard look at my life.

All my friends and classmates were getting ready for the Senior Prom, living a carefree life, living the best years of their lives. And here I was, living in a world of debt and disappointment with a man that I could barely stand being with. I was so confused, so unhappy, and so close to the edge.

What in the world of God had I gotten myself into? How could I have done this to myself? How could I make this okay?

I needed relief. I was so angry about the drapes, and the damage done to the wall of my bedroom. Honestly, I didn't understand it! However strange and abnormal my home with my parents was ... there was never any violence.

So, the next day, I confronted Brian about his childish destructive tantrums. I was reading him the riot act, when in the blink of an eye, he flew at me and began punching me everywhere. Much more than the physical beating that I took, and it was brutal … but so much more than that, the mental turmoil that ensued from that experience to this day leaves me close to despair when I think about it.

I have tendencies toward harmony and quiet in my life. And it's true that I did not relate to him. But I gave one hundred percent of myself to the marriage. I did my part. I did more than my part. I was, at this point, seventeen years old, and my life just kept getting darker. I really needed guidance!

Brian was very sorry, but we all know how that pattern plays out. If I stayed, I was condemning myself to a repetitive episodic torture chamber. If I left and went home, I had to face a future filled with "I told you so." I did not know how to function in the world on my own, and I was injured from the beating. I was in shock! Too shocked to cry. I had taken several blows to the head, and I knew that I was hurt. But, I was ashamed to seek help. So I stayed as still and quiet as possible, to try to assess any physical damage.

A day or two later, I packed some clothes and took my bruised body back home to "good ole Mom. " Dad happened to be there, so I got it with both barrels. Not once did either of them ask if I was okay. I had entered the very place that drove me out to begin with, and had walked through the door, defeated and lifeless, tail between my legs. Mom said, and I quote, "Well I don't know what to tell you. You better get yourself a job."

Dad went into a fiery rant, spewing out things like … "I told you not to marry that son of a bitch! What kind of a man punches a woman! I'd like to find the son of a bitch and punch him around!"

But there was no sympathy for me. No words of compassion like perhaps, "I'm so sorry this happened," or "It will be okay." Their pattern of thought was that I should pick up the pieces and get on with it. If there had ever been a small element of comfort for me in that house, it was gone. There was no sense of belonging within those walls at all. And certainly no sense of anyone reaching out or welcoming me.

Also ... any hint of a developing bond between Dad and me was eradicated completely. Instead, the tiny promise of an actual real connection, or dare I say friendship, had regressed into negative territory. Neither of my parents offered even a suggestion for a possible solution to the declining direction of my life.

My ability to feel was so inhibited from a lifetime that lacked encouragement or love, while my thought process was working overtime and was filled with static. I had not one iota of clarity in my head, and was in intense emotional pain. My existence seemed wretched and stark. After a week or maybe two, not knowing what to do, and desperate for relief, I was trying to think of a way to resurrect the marriage.

I was seventeen and free. I had survived my physical wounds. If I applied myself, I could have picked up the pieces and embarked on a productive life and career. (Of course, this is in hindsight.) I was desperate for guidance, and there was no guidance. I was completely on my own, as I had always been.

Flirting with disaster, once again,
I became a headless rider on a horse with no legs
—TLC

So within a month following the catastrophic fiasco over the drapes, back I went, into the dregs of hell. I reunited with

Brian. I would love to be able to say here at this juncture of my story that Brian came crawling back to me filled with remorse and vowing his undying love, promising a life of peace and harmony. That's not how it went, though. As I had done before, I willingly knocked on the door of adversity. To be honest, Brian was agreeable. No more, no less.

Upon returning to the apartment, I found that Brian had abandoned the place after I left. W.T. Grants came and took back all the furniture. So the place was barren and devoid of any traces of my sweet little fantasy life. The apartment complex came in and took everything that was left. They took treasures that I cherished, like letters from my parents' courtship, and baby books and baby shoes that were mine and my brother's. They took every trace of anything that I cared about and was defined by from my past. And they disposed of it all!

I had no happy future to look forward to. No sense of belonging in the present ... no pride ... not even a shred of self-respect. And now I had no evidence of a past.

If there was such a thing as a walking coma, that would have been me. I was completely empty, and beyond caring about it. I had no hopes, no plans, no ambition.

Brian and I now had no place to live. And even if we did, we had no furniture, no dishes, or pots and pans, no towels or sheets. We owned a failing 1961 Chevy, and all of our belongings fit into the back seat.

We took a furnished room about the size of a single garage, with a tiny kitchen set-up, a small bathroom, and a pull-out sofa. It also had a little black and white TV. Brian would go off to work in the morning, and I would remain under the covers of our couch bed, and watch cartoons all day. I went through very little motions that would indicate life. I was in a state of serious shock and depression. We ate a variety of fast food for dinners. We continued on like that for months.

In my entire marriage to Brian, there was one single night of genuine passion. It was in this little furnished room. I still can't say that our spirits actually became one; that never happened. Brian had no spirit, and he had no soul. But that one night, we engaged in long hot sex. It was actually good. And the next morning I felt a subtle awareness of a possible physical change. I remember distinctly thinking that I might be, pregnant. Morning sickness began within days, and the prospect of having a baby became a reality. I think we both looked forward to this new direction that our lives would take.

This, of course, brought up the dilemma of living somewhere, and preparing for our baby. We had nothing. We had no real options. My mother had restructured the back of her house into two rooms with private entrances, for the purpose of extra income, and the rest of the house was reduced to modest living quarters for her. She proposed to us that she should live in one of the back rooms, and Brian and I could move into the living quarters. We agreed upon a monthly rent, and we were to begin another interesting period of life.

Brian and I left our small furnished room. We left owing money.

I want to make something clear! This irresponsible behavior was not something I was brought up with. Both Mom and Dad were credible people. Bills got paid. Responsibilities were honored.

This reckless disregard for financial accountability was something I learned from Brian. I unlearned it as I got older. Unfortunately, it was — and still is — a way of life for Brian.

Other than a roof over my head, and a place to prepare for my baby, there was no plus side to living in that house with my mother. It was instead a constant reminder of my progression of tragic mistakes.

My father, upon learning of my pregnancy, completely gave up on me. After making it clear that he was not going to do the "Grampa thing," he pretty much ignored my existence. Mom still fucked him once in a while, and when she wasn't busy with that, she was making eyes at the gardener, a feeble slimy-looking thing who lived in the other rented room.

There was a door that opened from the hallway of the two back rooms into our living room. It was like a free-for-all for Mom. No knock, no greeting, just barging into my home anytime she pleased. After a while, I placed the sofa on the wall where the door was, to block access into my living area. I can still see the expression on her face when she opened the door with gusto, and it slammed into the back of the sofa. She was angry and annoyed. I thoroughly enjoyed it!

And so it went. I ate myself into oblivion throughout the pregnancy. I was very apprehensive about giving birth. There was no extraordinary care given to me because of my condition. It was clear to me that I was not, in any way, special. We bought and refinished second-hand nursery furniture. The most prevalent feeling that I can remember during this period of time, was "loneliness." I felt so intensely alone and hoped with all of my heart that the birth of my baby would somehow change our marriage for the better. I fantasized about Brian's anticipation and excitement in the hospital.

So, at the age of eighteen, I gave birth to my first child. I was hoping for a boy, and I did indeed have a son. I had been in labor at home for most of the day, and I was anxious and afraid. My mother kept telling me over and over: "Now remember, it has to get worse before it gets better!" That is a perfect example of how useless my mother was. I left for the hospital at eight in the evening. Brian checked me in and went home.

I was in this alone.

My son was born at two in the morning. The recovery room was a dark room with four beds, and I was the only occupant. I was wide awake, and there was a phone right next to my bed. There were no calls, and no husband. I stayed in that room until dawn, alone. The silent message that came to me was deafening. It said to me, "You don't matter at all, to anyone." By noon, I was past all reason. I couldn't believe that even Brian could be this insensitive. Would he ever come and hold me, and say I love you, and see his new baby? He showed up after two in the afternoon, all decked out in a shiny new gray suit and coat, and hat.

This day was not about us, and not about the baby.

This day was all about Brian!

We named our son Daniel.

I had developed a serious depression upon returning home. Brian left for a work-related five-day trip out of state. I was, again, in this alone. I remember having to go to the laundromat with a new infant. I had to pack the laundry, the baby, and the diaper bag into the car. I couldn't even fake a smile. I was tired and anxious, and I remember thinking that I will never go anywhere for the rest of my life without a diaper bag.

Time passed slowly, and I did my best with my boy. I kept him clean. I sterilized his bottles. I had wanted to breastfeed my baby, but Brian said no, that it wasn't natural ... so I didn't. Again, I want to clarify: All these decisions were agreed to, not because I was weak. I was never weak. I was completely oblivious. My life was becoming more and more complex, and I was totally void. I knew nothing about anything in life. I was so inexperienced that I couldn't even recognize my own instincts, let alone trust them. So I just followed along, going through the motions that seemed normal, and trying with all my might to be okay with my life, so that I could make my baby's life okay.

6

Simmering

And so life began for me as a mother! Danny was a good natured baby. It was time for me to accept my imperfect life, and make it as good as possible.

I had to stop longing for a life where I would be cherished, appreciated, and encouraged. I had to try to somehow give myself support and learn to trust my feelings and decisions. There was another life in the balance now, and Brian was an absolute hands-*off* father. He probably liked his son. I say like because I don't believe Brian knew then or now, how to love anyone or anything, including himself. Brian's needs always came first. But okay, at this point, I certainly knew that!

I was down on myself, as well, because as much as I did all my domestic duties, and I fulfilled all my motherly tasks and responsibilities with as much enthusiasm as I could muster up, I knew deep down that I should have been more present in Danny's life.

We left my mother's house within weeks after Danny was born and rented a dilapidated house in the same town. I was getting around to doctor visits, the laundromat, and grocery store, with my infant son, in a car with no brakes. So that when I wanted the car to stop, I needed to carefully work the brake pedal, which would create a ringing noise from the brake to rotor contact; while pulling up on the emergency brake to assist.

A short time after we moved into that house, the stove went, and I was cooking three meals a day on a single hot plate.

My quest during that time was simply ... personal survival. If my thought process extended itself past that, I knew that I would lose my mind.

Brian had a bit of a checkered past, but it wasn't something that I made public, and it came to my attention that he had spilled it all to some close friends. I was terribly embarrassed by this. Brian had agreed not to expose his past to anyone, and as usual, I rediscovered that Brian's word meant nothing. Now I would just have to live with the fact that our business was "out there." I would merely add this to the long list of other betrayals. Upon this discovery, however, I proceeded to confront him, and express my disdain for his lack of any consideration for my feelings. I was not agitated. I was hurt. I was not shouting. My tone was one notch above "matter of fact." He was lying on the left side of the bed. I was sitting on the bottom right facing him as I spoke. Suddenly, his right foot plunged forward and struck me in the forehead. The blow made full contact, and it was so hard that I did a backwards flip and landed across the room on the floor. It took me awhile to process what had happened. I would have preferred death, rather than surviving this assault, and having to learn to live with yet another humiliating beating at the hands of what I came to regard as a spineless coward.

As I had done in the past, I initiated a reconciliation. I just could not face my parents again with a failed marriage. I couldn't face it myself! How in the world would I live on my own, and now with a baby? Brian couldn't even support me living in the same house. I knew that financial support after a break up was a fantasy. More importantly, I did not want my marriage to fail. It was the only decisive move I had ever made in my life. I was hopeful that as we put the years behind us, we would grow closer.

I just wanted the fairy-tale scenario. I wanted it so desperately!

At this point in my life, I think I was at my lowest level in terms of self worth, and it was during this time period that one last intensely painful development occurred before I began to take hold of myself. Even though I remained so naive, and still clung to the prospect of a marriage that held to somewhat of a customary standard, the following event turned me inside out.

If Brian was or had been unfaithful to me, I guess the idea of it bothered me, but in reality, I couldn't even understand how anyone would want him. I mean I "had" to be physical with him, but if I could choose a lover just from what little experience I had, I never would have chosen Brian. I resigned myself to the sad truth that I, through no one's fault but my own, was saddled with Brian, and was destined to live out my days with a disappointing, unsatisfying, passionless man. In my mind, I had accepted the fact that my sex life was forever doomed. But as I have stated before, I would honor the commitment I made to him.

Soon after Danny's birth, and around the time of Brian's last physical assault on me — while I was driving in a brakeless car, and cooking on a hot plate — I noticed that Brian and my fifteen-year-old cousin Violet had eyes for each other. He would look at her with puppy-dog eyes, and she (the daughter of my mother's brother ... someone with whom we shared holidays and family gatherings), was readily receptive. This was a shocking and a brutal display for me to watch. And it was blatant! I wasn't the only one who could see it. After a while, my uncle had to get involved and intervene. And there was never even a hint of an apology from my cousin. Even after years and years went by, the unspoken message from Violet was not in the least contrite, but instead, "Yup ... that's how it was, and so what?" There was no regard for my dignity or concern for the humiliation that Violet contributed to. And as for Brian, what was he thinking? Violet was a small-minded, arrogant self-centered cow!

That was a tough nut to crack for me. But I was so good at living in denial. Even at family get-togethers, I was able to make believe that the despicable behavior of those two people simply never happened.

In my life, that was an ugly ordeal that I never completely recovered from. And the way I handled it, or more accurately "didn't" handle it, remains one of my biggest disappointments in myself. Nothing that happened between Brian and me after that cut so deep. It was that experience that raised my threshold for pain. And it was after that incident that I began to question my values, and ask myself how much more I was willing to endure for the sake of a normal appearance.

If you step onto a train heading into a long journey, and begin to realize that the train is taking you to the wrong place ... do you stay on to the end? Or do you get off at the next stop and find the train that will take you where you should be going?

At this point, I had a six-month-old baby and could not jump off while the train was in motion. But even though it was not exactly clear to me at the time, I was on the lookout for the next stop.

7

Twilight

Time marched on. Brian and I had moved about fifty miles out East. I don't remember how we did it, but we bought a big spit-level home. By the grace of God, the mortgage was approved. I would guess that Danny was about thirteen months old at the time. The house was beautiful. This was a young area with all new homes.

Low and behold! It turned out that Brian was a person with a full-fledged green thumb. He established a beautiful lush green lawn and kept it perfectly manicured. And I should add that Brian was a gifted vegetable gardener, as well.

This chapter of our lives had a whisper of normalcy to it, and I was drinking it up. The neighborhood was filled with young families. We were part of a growing community, all eager to know one another. Everyone took pride in his home and family. There were many Friday night gatherings and summer block parties.

This was the most defined sense of belonging that I had experienced since high school. It was a happy time for us.

So ... everyone in the neighborhood was having a new baby, and you guessed it! We went for it! It took us three months to nail down pregnancy number two. Now, as I approached the age of twenty-one, I felt calmer about the prospect of a new baby. My children would be just under three years apart, and I looked forward to the upcoming addition to our family. Morning sickness was right on schedule, and I was tired all the time. I once again ate myself into oblivion. And life went on month to month.

Late in the pregnancy, we were missing our old familiar neighborhood once again, and another move was in the wind. During this time period, there was a good deal of emotional upheaval. Brian was out often for job estimates. He may or may not have been unfaithful; I did not keep tabs on him. There had been enough turmoil in my life.

There was a neighbor down the road, Shirley Capadora. She was married to the sweetest man, and had two adorable boys. She was condescending and cruel to her husband. I felt sorry for him. Shirley had her eye on most of the men she knew. I was once again so naive. We were friends as a couple, and it never entered my mind that a friend would make an unrelenting play for my husband. But she did, and Brian enjoyed every minute of it.

Cheating was bad enough. But cheating with a neighbor, or friend, or as in my previous experience with a family member, in an unabashed display for all to see, is cruel. It is particularly cruel when your spouse is getting wind of it, and moreover when your wife is seven months' pregnant. To be honest though ... this bothered me more at the level of pride than anything else. I had been down this road before, and it was old news. And more importantly, I thought Shirley Capadora was crazy to even want Brian, and that she would be really sorry that she had pursued this avenue with him, about five minutes after they got their clothes off. In fact, the biggest favor that she could have done for me, would have been to steal Brian.

Also, at this time, during a routine conversation, I said something that Brian did not like. It was nothing out of the ordinary — just household type of talk — but maybe with a little attitude. Brian came at me fast and furious, and I ran for my life. I was hugely pregnant! He stopped before he got to me, but here I was back into that ugly bleak and menacing territory. When that occurred, I knew for sure that our marriage was alive on borrowed time. That I was so sick of being afraid. And that of the two of us, I was the only real person. I felt an inner strength and self-respect rising.

I had thrown away my most carefree years for Brian. I never belittled or showed him an ounce of disrespect. I swallowed a lot of shit, and had been through enough torment. I did not even know what pride was anymore, And here he is running after me to beat me, when I am seven months' pregnant. How brave would he be if I were a man, physically equal to him? ... *I was married to a slug!* And I was no longer eager to see this marriage through.

I could not think about the prospect of ending my marriage now, though. I wanted to move back down island, and I wanted to be in a calm rested condition when my new baby was born.

Our move was as bizarre as all the other moves we had made. We found a sweet little house and began the paper work to buy it. We were waiting to hear if the mortgage was approved. I had a good feeling about this house. It had a calm and tranquil quality to it.

One Sunday morning, we woke up and decided to move that day. Even though we had not yet been approved for a mortgage, the house was vacant, and we had the key. We packed up and left. We left so fast that our breakfast was still in the oven. Two days later, there were curtains in the windows of our little house. I was getting good at this!

Our big house out east became the house with nobody in it. We had no idea what to do with it, and we were way too busy loving our new place, and preparing for the new baby to even care. Thank God, the paperwork was approved.

My doctor and hospital were out east, so I would be having the baby out there. Two realtors made us an offer on the big house. We chose the one that would be the quickest.

A few days later, I went into labor during the morning, and I could not reach Brian. My mother drove me out to the hospital, and took Danny back home with her. Brian showed up late that afternoon, stayed for twenty minutes, then left to get something to eat. I had no expectations, no grandiose illusions of his being in the hospital for the birth. This was not my first rodeo … I knew the drill.

I gave birth to a little girl at just after nine that evening. When they brought her in to me and I held her, it was magical. She was adorable. She was beautiful. We named her Elizabeth!

Everyone was delighted to welcome a girl. People came from far and wide to see her. It was a happier time for me than my first birth. I was still young, only twenty-one, but twenty-one was way more mature than eighteen. I was more settled within myself, and it made me a little sad that Danny was born at such a tumultuous time. After Elizabeth's birth,

I was in the hospital for two or three days. Brian would drive out after work. I didn't know it at the time, but he would sit with me until visiting hours were over. Then he would spend a couple of hours with Shirley Capadora before going home.

What a guy!

Upon returning home with Elizabeth, I fell into a good solid routine. Having two children was enjoyable. I did not experience any depression, and I enjoyed watching the children interact. I loved living in that house, and I was more in control of my life than ever before.

As usual, the car we were driving at the time was falling apart. Every bill was paid late or never. This was the norm for us. I was miserable living like this, but had no control over it. Even when I took over the budget, Brian would give me the remainder of his salary after he had indulged himself with new fishing gear, or whatever struck his fancy at that moment. And I could not stretch what he gave me far enough.

My mother bailed us out several times and provided jackets or shoes for the kids, and I can't tell you how much fun that was … Mom's eyes rolling and her comments about her saintly gestures, and what a pain in the ass I was. I wanted to tell her to go fuck herself, but who was I kidding? … She was right! I don't know what I would have done without her help. I did recognize that. But it would have been nice if she didn't make me eat it each time.

So Brian's reckless disregard for any semblance of responsible living created a dependence on my mother, which provided her with an unending state of martyrdom. This very unpleasant condition became a way of life. I made the best of it, although I couldn't imagine how Brian could so blatantly accept this display of his own failure to take care of his family.

One afternoon, I was going out for milk. I was making a fast run, because Brian needed the car that night. Just around the block, I happened to see a familiar car. What are the odds that at that precise moment, Shirley Capadora, my neighbor from out east, fifty miles away would be here, around the block from my house? I sincerely believed that an incredible coincidence had occurred. I stopped by her car and said, "Oh my God, you're not going to believe this, but I live on the next block over!" TRULY, this is what I thought! I invited her over, but she declined. I then went home and said to Brian, "You are not going to believe this, but guess who I ran into around the block?"

This was who I was, and may still be who I am. I am not a manipulator, and I don't contrive. I never have, and I never will. There is such a thing as discretion. It is beyond me, no matter what deed was in the wind, how two people could be so careless and uncaring about stripping away someone's dignity. My dignity. Why couldn't they have made a mature discreet plan? And not only that, I didn't know what was going on that night. I didn't get it at all. But then one day … *I got it!*

I saw the whole convoluted, immature story of the night that Shirley Capadora was waiting for Brian, around the block from my house. Was I in shock? To tell you the truth, maybe I was in shock for a moment. But mostly I felt sorry for Shirley's husband. As for me, a strange thing was happening to me.

I thought carefully, and in great depth about Brian. I don't know how many times Brian was unfaithful to me, or with how many women, but after my cousin Violet and now Shirley Capadora, it was pretty obvious to me that the sooner I got away from this useless fuck, the sooner I could begin my life.

> *How many times do you have to get hit over the head*
> *before you figure out who's hitting you?*
> —Harry Truman

After this latest development. I was seeing my life from a broader platform. I was incredulous. It wouldn't be long now before I took hold of my destiny. I was sure of this.

There were several times that I had considered taking a lover. I had often wondered what real sex—sex with passion—would be like. I can honestly say that being unfaithful is not something that appealed to me. It would be cheating for the sake of cheating, and that is not where I wanted to go. Although, at this point, I could easily call it something else. I could think of it as an exercise in self-respect, or self-preservation … even just survival.

There was no integrity at all in my marriage. None. And it's likely that there never had been. But I was sure that there was integrity inside of me. It was something I genuinely liked about myself. Anyway, there was no one that I could think of with whom I wanted to have an affair, so the whole idea was moot.

8

Epiphany

So I went along in the day-to-dayness of my life. I was married to a man who was a billboard for incompetence, with no honesty, brains, savvy, ambition or responsibility. He couldn't even cheat with any class. He lived on the surface, and his most developed talent was instant gratification. The mortgage was behind; the electric bill was late. This was like a never-ending nightmare. I was sickened by the sight of him.

I was apprehensive, though. I had two children. If I were on my own, how would I feed them? How could I work, and still be with them? And I loved my little house. Where would I go? Time moved along, and the instability of my life remained consistent. But for the first time, I was experiencing ongoing personal growth. I was acutely aware of this. My confidence grew gradually and steadily. I felt stronger and stronger as the days passed. And more importantly, the more I saw myself, the more I liked myself.

Household chores became less important, and spending time with the children took precedence. I took increased pride in my clothes and appearance. My new powerful and ever-growing inner strength became more than obvious … it was glaring. Brian was more attentive toward me every day. He seemed unsure of the state of our marriage. And with good reason! At this point, he could have sprouted wings, and it wouldn't have made the slightest bit of difference to me.

One afternoon, I found Brian in the garage, smoking pot. He was up front about it, and wanted me to try it. I knew that many of my cousins had smoked it, and I agreed to have them all over, and give marijuana a try.

This experience was monumental in my life!

It was a Friday evening. The children were in bed. Everyone arrived about eight o'clock. I was apprehensive, and had no idea what to expect. I was inexperienced with alcohol, but assumed that the effects would be similar. Joints were rolled, and then were passed around. My cousin's husband was helpful with the procedure. "Take it in to your lungs as deep as possible, and hold it for as long as you can." So I followed his instructions. I took one or two hits, and soon realized that a broad grin was fixed on my face, and my first thought was, *Great day in the morning!* It became apparent to me that not only was I incredibly happy, but everyone was happy. Happy and really laughing. Laughing and eating. Eating anything they could find.

It was so fine for the first few minutes, and then a most curious and intense experience occurred. I saw myself and my life with absolute and undeniable clarity. Though enlightening, it was terrifying. All the wrong choices that I had made came into view. The life I was living was a lie. Every truth inside of me had been abandoned, because I had not found the courage to face reality. I became so afraid. I wondered if this intense high would ever end. *What if it didn't? Maybe I should go to the hospital and get an antidote!*

So as everyone in my house was having a grand time, I went into my bedroom and got into bed under the covers. I thought, *I'll just lie here very still until I feel more normal.* As I was waiting for the high to wear off, and through my trepidation, I began to assess this new state of mind.

First of all, I knew for sure that if I could control it, this new consciousness would be great! I had seen the cold hard truth about myself, and my life. Once you see something so profound, you can't unsee it. So now it was a matter of simply becoming the person that I was born to be, or live in denial for the rest of my life. I definitely wanted more glimpses of myself. I was completely receptive to this as a source of enjoyment, and a tool for emotional evolution.

Brian and I went about our lives normally, but began smoking pot once or twice a week. I had discovered that music was profoundly more beautiful and pleasurable after smoking. And I would find myself planning different sets of music to listen to when I got high.

All of my senses were enhanced, and the best part was that they remained enhanced, to some extent, after the high was over, as well. I guess once you hear something beautiful, you can't unhear it.

After viewing all of the deep dimensions of myself, I decided to realize and live in the new depth that my most prevalent core beliefs were now dictating.

It is an interesting little afterthought that Brian did not share this profound enlightenment with me. He just smoked, and laughed, and ate; but he never saw the things that I saw. Who cared, though? Not me! Turning my life around would be work, but it would also be well worth the effort. I would do the work!

It is not death that a man should fear,
but he should fear never beginning to live.
— Marcus Aurelius

9

An Unexpected Pleasure

Brian began to talk often about a Norwegian fellow named Erik whom he had met on the job. Brian was in awe of Erik's talent and knowledge. This was all Brian talked about: "Erik this" and "Erik that."

Brian wanted to build a fancy closet upstairs in our house and asked Erik to help him. So this great, intelligent, genius carpenter was coming over to apply his expertise in woodworking to our upstairs closet.

Erik was a tall, blond, blue-eyed enigma to me. I had never experienced such charisma. And no man had ever looked at me the way Erik looked at me. I suddenly loved the sound of a Norwegian accent. Brian asked me, "So what do you think … isn't he great?"

Erik came over many times in the evenings. He would sit at the kitchen table with Brian for hours at a time, and sip brandy, and talk into the wee hours of the morning about a various array of topics. Erik was Brian's hero. I did not go out of my way to be part of this. I had no interest in involving myself in their conversation. But if Erik passed by close to me, or I to him, I would receive a quick unmistakable glance. There was no doubt that I was beginning to fantasize about Erik. Sexual fantasy was new to me, and I was simply and innocently having fun with it.

Then, one day when Brian was not home, the phone rang. It was Erik. Erik said, "Will you meet me somewhere?"

I replied, "You tell me where to be, and I'll be there!"

There were no games, no lurking around, no snickering, no puppy dog eyes, no attempt to belittle Brian. We simply met at a hotel and made love. Yes, I made love to someone for the first time in my life. It was grand, and then it was over. I loved the entire experience, and I loved the way it was handled. This was not an act of revenge, although the circumstances of Brian and Erik's friendship made this especially satisfying.

When I got home, I wished I could have said to Brian: *"Now that's how it's done!"*

So life in my marriage continued on. I was still looking for an opening in which to escape. And my self-confidence continued to grow with each passing day. I trusted my instincts completely. This was all so new for me.

Our financial status became worse, and I was seriously concerned. Now the mortgage was three months' behind. Brian just plodded along in his familiar irresponsible pattern. He became more and more aware of my personal growth, and I don't think he was thrilled about it. Brian went through a couple of periods of remorse, though I never knew exactly what was behind the remorse, and I never asked. At that point, I didn't care. My guess was that he knew that our relationship for all intents and purposes was over.

The plain truth is that the only reason I was with him, was that I was stuck with him, and I couldn't figure a way out. I had two children, and we had to live somewhere. The success of my marriage was no longer a viable issue to me. In fact, there was no way to bring it back. There was nothing Brian could do or say.

If Brian was anxious or sad about the loss that was facing him, it was not because he cared about me, or all the torment I went through because of him. It was not because he was losing someone that he loved. It was simply because he couldn't be alone. It wasn't that he needed me; he didn't even know me. Brian just needed someone.

10

A Clean Break

Danny was approaching his first day of kindergarten. We were all geared up for his big day. Thanks to my mother, he had a wonderful wardrobe to wear during his first year of school. Elizabeth was now two years old and toddling around. Brian's temper was in check for the most part; but the sad truth is that I lived my life walking on egg shells. There was always an underlying level of fear that now extended to the children.

One night, Brian was particularly severe disciplining Danny, because Danny had woken up and would not go back to sleep. It wasn't that Brian was unreasonably harsh, but I could always feel the dark undertone, and I was so sick of the stress every time Brian raised his voice. He slapped Danny. Danny was crying. I had reached the point of overflow.

I simply looked at Brian and said, "I want you to leave." Brian would never lower himself to ask why, or consider groveling, and I'm sure that he was thinking that he would punish me for questioning his authority.

He replied, "Fine," and walked out!

The unexpected excitement that I felt at that moment was indescribable. Was this going to be the beginning of my life?

We did not own a suitcase, so I began packing Brian's clothes into black trash bags. I felt like doing the "dance of joy," but I had a long way to go in order to actually define this moment. The buildup of courage and strength and determination that I was feeling was equal to launching a missile to the stars. There would be no second thoughts this time. I was more than willing to face the failure. I knew that I would have to come up with some kind of a plan ... and quickly! I had to somehow figure out a way to provide for the kids. But ... I was completely sure that I would rather live in the street and eat bread and water, than spend one more day with Brian. That is to say that no matter how difficult life would be now, it would be glorious without Brian.

> *I would rather die on my feet,*
> *than live on my knees.*
> — Euripides

Brian came back two days later, with a chip on his shoulder, expecting the same old drill: Waiting for me to signal him that eventually we would get past this. My God! He was such an arrogant man. There he stood thinking that he controlled my entire universe.

All of his clothes were packed, and the black trash bags were neatly lined up. It didn't take too long for him to realize that this time it was different. It was over! There was nothing to talk about. I didn't want to smirk. I didn't want to gloat. I didn't want to argue, insult or offend him. I just wanted him out!

I had thought about how I would survive, and I knew that child support would be tenuous at best. I suggested to him that he sign the failing and almost foreclosed house over to me in exchange for alimony, which I knew he would never pay anyway.

I needed a place to raise Danny and Elizabeth, and I loved my house. If I could somehow salvage it, I would; and I had nothing to lose by trying. I wanted this done immediately, as well as a legal separation drawn up and witnessed by an attorney.

That's how it played out. He was to give me a total of forty dollars a week (not even enough to pay for the children's lunches). But I didn't care, as long as he was gone. The house would be mine if and when I got the mortgage paid up to date. There were two liens against the house from the oil company and the electric company. I had my work cut out for me!

My mother and father happened by one night during this most compelling transition in my life.

Dad and I went outside and sat in the car, and I brought him up to date. He calmly said to me, "You made your bed; now you lay in it. And by the way, don't think your mother is going to watch your kids for you."

I thought to myself, *hmmmmmmm, not getting any emergency help there!*

But honestly, I didn't care. As long as Brian was out of my life, nothing else mattered.

I upgraded my driver's license to a Class E, and drove a cab endless hours at a time. My brother's wife looked after the kids when I was in a pinch. I borrowed money from my mother, and watched her eyes roll and listened to her tell me that I was pain in the ass. It was okay! It was all okay, as long as Brian was gone!

It took a long time for things to level off, but they did. Brian's support checks over the years were often post dated, and I held my breath each time I cashed one. But mostly they went through.

Brian never provided medical insurance of any kind for us, and he did not provide any for the children now. This was a constant source of worry for me. Medical expenses just for minor care was a huge financial stretch, and I lived in fear of possible medical emergencies. This remained an enormous concern for me throughout Danny's and Elizabeth's childhood years.

11

Self Discovery

There were many issues in my life that demanded my attention, and needed to be addressed. Although, I longed for the carefree years that I had thrown away, I knew that attempting to rediscover my youth would be not only irresponsible, but counterproductive. I was twenty-three, with a full agenda, and two children to raise.

I never liked drinking alcohol, and the bar scene didn't appeal to me as a social outlet. Being pretty confident, I knew who I was, and did not need my ego stroked by men who might happen into my life.

I saw my two children for the first time as whole people and felt that my priorities with my time needed to be focused primarily on them. My son took the separation and forthcoming divorce hard. He began acting out. I spent a great deal of time and effort trying to make things okay for him, but I always remained on course. Danny was hopeful for the first year or two that his father might come back home. I told him time after time, as gently as I could, that it was never going to happen.

There were boundaries in our home. Rules to be realized and followed. The most prominent house rules that I insisted upon were "Honesty" and "Always taking responsibility for your own actions." As far as I could see, my children had only one shot of developing good solid values, and applying them to their lives. That one shot was me.

I gave this one hundred percent of myself. It was first and foremost in my mind. It was the most important thing that I would ever do, and I was always aware that there were two lives in the balance.

Did I do this most important job well? Did I succeed? Was I a good mother? Well I wish I could say "yes" ... beyond a shadow of a doubt, "yes." But it is not so cut and dry. I can say that I held tight to my beliefs, one thousand percent, but I was hard on the children. I ran a tight ship.

There was no other place, and no other person that would take the time and effort to insist on discipline and respect. And without discipline and respect for themselves and others, how would they survive in the world?

> *Let parents then bequeath to their children*
> *Not riches, but the spirit of reverence.*
> — Plato

I was frustrated by the fact that because I was the parent, demanding responsible behavior, I was the bad guy!

Their father dutifully saw them once a week. They watched him act like a teenager with young women. They witnessed his superficial values and desires for instant gratification. He had nothing to say to them that was constructive or reassuring. I had no control over this. All I could do was try to demonstrate, as best I could, how to be positive and productive.

At the time that this was all taking place, there was a stigma associated with divorce. Men readily complained about their demanding, and annoying "ex wives." And women were critically observed. Again, it took a little while before I was recognized and respected by everyone ... "in full measure" ... for the person that I was.

That is everyone except Brian, who never quite knew what to make of his complacent former wife, who turned into a fireball of ambition. He said whatever he could, to whoever would listen, including our children, to bring me down.

> *Positioned carefully beneath your rock,*
> *eyes darting back and forth*
> *You are cocked and loaded*
> *I stand tall in full view,*
> *unaffected by your distorted moral scope*
> *So take your best shot!*
> *—TLC*

Brian was confounded by my success, while he remained a small little person, incapable of even paying a bill on time.

During this time, I was fortunate enough to become part of a group of friends who shared my values, my goals, my fears, and my pleasures. All of us enjoyed a heightened awareness of the simple pleasures of life. We were supportive and caring, while respecting personal boundaries. There were no demands or expectations—just the enjoyment of one another's company. I trusted them completely.

These friends would become one of the most meaningful and treasured parts of my young life. The memories and adventures that we shared would last a lifetime! There were several men in this group. My relationship with all of them, while intimate, was platonic.

As I look back, I guess I inadvertently compartmentalized my life into well-defined categories. There were children, friends, work, and school, and a lover who provided me with the most exciting, passionate, adventurous sex imaginable.

I loved my home. It was ideal for me and the kids. It was "our" home, and I respected it as such. I never brought a man into my home. My children never woke up to find any strange "uncles" lying around or sitting at the kitchen table in their underwear. I made a point of this! Our home was sacred. It was for the three of us alone!

My sex life was outstanding, and I was madly in love with an extraordinary man. He was married, and I'm not particularly proud of that, but I'm telling the truth here. And that's the way it was. He cared for me and showed his love for me in a million different ways. I leaned on him emotionally, and it felt so good to be able to trust someone that much. He knew me, and was aware of the miserable years of my marriage, and suggested that I take the time to get to know myself a little, and think about what I wanted to do with my life. He did not ask to be part of the household or impinge upon my life in any way. He covered expenses that came up that I could not handle. Making love to him was the most fulfilling physical and emotional experience of give and take that I would ever know.

The most profound gift that he gave me was the finest and most caring gift of my entire life: He gave me a chance to catch my breath. He gave me the gift of time. We were together for four years.

I have had wonderful caring lovers in my life, and enjoyed being with them all. But no one came close to this man, who shall remain nameless. He took everything that I needed to give. My desire for him was never ending. He was the love of my life. And I will be grateful for the time we spent together until the day I die.

> *I miei ricordi sono tesori. Sarò sempre tua.*
> —TLC

It is interesting ... I had assumed that I would re-marry at some point in my life, although I never carried that thought much further. But in the back of my mind, the thought existed, not as a plan, just an assumption. However, the longer that I was on my own, the more I liked it. My life was good. My home was quiet. My pleasures were simple.

Bringing up the children and deciding on a career was challenging. And though a little hectic, my life had balance. I dated and enjoyed it. But I often found myself opting to stay home, cooking and just sitting in the quiet comfort of home's healing atmosphere. Home was my favorite place, day or night, winter or summer. It was where my heart and soul dwelled. I was never lonely!

Personally, I did not want the drama of an ongoing relationship. Maybe I was a little brain damaged from the seven years of the destructive marriage that I had endured; but nevertheless, my life now felt complete.

I longed to change my name back to my father's name, but that would have been opening up another can of worms. The house and all the bills were in my married name, and

I had developed an exemplary credit history. My school records and degrees were in my married name.

My major hesitation, though, was my two children, particularly my son. He had been wounded by the break-up to begin with. I felt as though he would interpret this as a statement saying, "I didn't like your father, and I don't like your name" … so I would wait as many years as I felt was necessary.

I didn't pay much attention to Brian's activities. As long as his child support checks cleared, and were up to date, I didn't care what he did or said. The relief of having him out of my life was like being on a continual high.

Brian remarried two or three years after our split. This was great for me, because it meant going forward from a legal separation to a final divorce. I was all for it.

Bridgett, his future wife, was Catholic, and she arranged for a priest to call me and request that I agree to an annulment. I wondered if they had planned to tell God that his children grew on trees. It's curious that she wanted a clean slate, and I was happy to cooperate, and did. Bridgett would never know, however, that Brian was married before me, that this marriage was number three for him.

So Brian and Bridgett had a grand wedding. They bought a house about eight miles from me, and the routine for the kids was that Brian would pick them up on Fridays after work, and return them back home Saturday morning before work. Very often, this amounted to an eight thirty or nine o'clock pick-up Friday evening, and a six o'clock drop back home Saturday morning. I truly felt sorry for Danny and Elizabeth. They barely had enough time to scoff down hamburgers from Roy Rogers fast food, get to bed, and then get up and come home. Brian did take them for a whole weekend once or twice a year.

Bridgett was a decent human being. She was not someone I would have chosen for a friend, but she was a nice woman. I felt so sorry for her because she stuck herself with Brian. It wasn't long before I would see resentment in her eyes toward me; not because I was better than she, not because I had a lifestyle that she envied, but because I was free of Brian, and she was stuck with him!

Brian played the role of a victimized divorced husband every time an opportunity presented itself. It was as if he were playing some make believe game. But he was playing it by himself.

I made a point of having the children remember his birthday. I bought and wrapped gifts for him and Bridgett from Danny and Elizabeth on Christmas. I sent the children to his home with gifts for Bridgett on Mother's Day.

My train of thought was wanting my children to feel like they had three people who loved them now, rather than two. Just as a point of interest, none of this was ever reciprocated.

I felt sad for Bridgett because she had wanted children of her own, and never had any. Whether Brian and Bridgett did or didn't have a family together was none of my business or concern, but I was more than willing to have my children recognize Bridgett as an auxiliary parent. Danny and Elizabeth were free to love her if they wished. I did not feel threatened one little bit.

Those years of raising the children in that sweet little house were good years for me. The gravity of the life that I provided for them, the choices I made for them, the answers to questions they asked about life, their options in the world, and the consequences of their actions, weighed heavier on me than any other aspect of my life. I would lie awake many nights hoping that I said the right words, hoping that any wisdom that I had acquired would be an aid to their developing perception of right and wrong. I'm sure that I made a million mistakes.

What I'm saying is that my concern for Danny's and Elizabeth's well-being was behind every action I took and every word I said. This was the only area of my life where I second guessed myself.

In life, you can only do what you believe to be right.

I was very young. In some ways this was a great benefit to my relationship with my children. But in some ways it was a negative, because I was growing up in conjunction with them. Being a mother was mind boggling!

I had dated a man on and off for a couple of years. He and I shared many of the same values. He was divorced and had two young daughters about the same age as Danny and Elizabeth. I was not madly in love with him, but I genuinely liked him a lot, and thought there was potential for us as time went by. Because we both had busy schedules, the time we spent together was limited. His ex-wife went into a massive cardiac arrest and died at the young age of thirty-three. This tragic event threw his life into a whole different dimension. He took his girls in to live with him and had to think seriously about the ramifications of full-time parenting, while working a full-time career.

This was a bit of a crossroad for me also. If I wanted to have the white picket fence fantasy come true, I could have a shot at it now. We were a good couple. If I married him, I would have someone to share my life with. We could be a real family with four children. His girls were sweet and easy to be with, but they had been through so much already. They had lost their mother! They would now unquestionably need a woman in their lives who could confidently take them under her wing, and help them along, while giving them the support they needed.

I could not commit to this for so many reasons. I worried day and night about mothering my own two children. The moral responsibility of four was overwhelming just thinking about it. I didn't feel like I gave my own two enough of myself, and this would have cut that time in half.

I had also become involved in metallurgy. I was studying the science and physical properties of metal alloys, and the relationship of their different components to each other. I had been acquiring credits towards certification; and I was working a small laboratory, single handed. I worked from nine to three each day, which had given me time to have a real life with my children. My work schedule allowed me to come home at the same time Danny and Elizabeth got home from school. I was able to cook a good meal, and we sat down to dinner every night as a family.

In addition to this most peaceful and productive period of my life to date, my job had great potential for a comfortable living in the future. It had taken me years to format life on my own. I liked the path I was on. So I backed away from any prospect of change and possible instability.

Now, for the first time, I had fully realized the distinct likelihood that I might never remarry.

12

Danny

Months turned to years, and the years passed — and we, all three of us, grew. All my well thought-out strategies for raising honest, happy, healthy and strong children who would have the desire and ability to give, and the pleasure of taking, barely made it to the finish line alive.

There was no such thing as a sure thing, a proven technique or a worry-free plan to raise well-adjusted children. I discovered, and rediscovered this frustrating sad truth, a thousand times.

Danny and I would butt heads often. He did listen to me once in a while; but more often than not, he didn't, and I would reach the "boiling over" point. Danny knew me well enough to recognize that the point of no return was fast approaching, and I was always surprised that when I was close to the edge with anger … he would simply give me that little extra push over.

Danny spent a great deal of time writing "I must not this, and I must not do that." We began at a fifty-time repetition, but by the end of his childhood, we were up into the thousands. "Did that work? you ask." No! I'm not even sure that it gave him pause before his next insubordinate shenanigan. I often felt as though he and I invented a game called "Who can be more stubborn."

A major problem in my interaction with my son was that my parenting was often affected by guilt. I was so ridiculously young when he was born. I did not receive him with open arms. And I was so confused by the state of my own life, that I didn't even recognize his birth for the gift that it was. In addition, the first two or three years of his life were filled with turmoil and unhappiness. My heart breaks when I think about it, but I can't go back and change the circumstances. I overcompensated for this during his childhood, perhaps projecting an apologetic energy toward him. Maybe that hint of remorse empowered him in a negative way. I was also filled with guilt because of the split-up with his father.

Whatever the reason for his relentless and adamant challenge to my authority, I could not break through the barrier.

My biggest concern was whether or not he would be able to go out into the world and follow the rules of society so that he could make a decent living and provide himself with a good life.

The other side of the coin was that Danny was smart and fun to be with. He was sweet, and he was a great worker. When he did his chores around the house, he was fast and thorough. I could always recognize the good as well as the bad, but the fact remained that following orders was not his strong suit. And that just kept getting worse.

At age seventeen, I took him to the Naval Recruiting Office. He signed up and though I was sad, I felt it would be exactly what he needed. There was no war. He could get as much of an education as he desired. He would have money in his pocket. And he could see the world and nurture his adventurous spirit. And so he was off! He would call me from time to time and say, "I can't thank you enough for making me do this. I love it," or "How could you have done this to me? I hate it," depending on which way the wind was blowing that day.

Later in his life, Danny became successful on the path he chose. He is hard working, dependable, responsible, a great cook and much more. And for this I am very proud. Sadly though, we never got past the personal friction from years before. And that has raised its ugly head intermittently through the years.

In my opinion, Danny still feels like he got short changed, or that he would have liked a more conventional life and mother. Years later, we were still butting heads. Danny tends to lash out just enough to make a hurtful point, but not enough to acknowledge his aggression. He takes my own words, thoughts and beliefs and tries to use them in a mental combat with me. But the bottom line is:

Nobody can be me – better than me!

The pattern of my life has clearly shown that I can bang my head against the wall over and over for a long time; then just simply conclude, in the blink of an eye, without a shadow of a doubt, that I have had enough!

Danny and Elizabeth were incredibly different. Their needs were different—their ambition and drive, musical preferences, appetite for life, level of compassion, capacity for love, and degree of sensitivity. Not one better than the other; just essentially different. There was a great deal of sibling rivalry over my attention.

I could be wrong, but I did not see a whole lot of depth in Danny's relationship with his father. On occasion, he would go to work with Brian, and after work, they would go to a local pub, where Danny would fill up on cherry cokes. Danny did love Brian; I just didn't see a notable parallel plane between them.

. . .

If you can talk with crowds and keep your virtue,
Or walk with kings — nor lose the common touch,
If neither foes nor loving friends can hurt you,
If all men count with you, but none too much;
If you can fill the unforgiving minute
With sixty seconds' worth of distance run,
Yours is the Earth and everything that's in it,
And — which is more — you'll be a Man, my son!
—Rudyard Kipling

13

Elizabeth

It seemed to me that Elizabeth melded more with her father. Brian loved to fish, and so did Elizabeth. They had become fishing buddies. I think that when you're sitting in a small boat for hours, with your line out in the water, there would have to be meaningful conversation or meaningful silence.

The first thirteen or fourteen years of Elizabeth's life were delightful. And being the first girl to arrive in my family after a long line of boys, she was spoiled by everyone. She tended to be lazy and sloppy (sloppy would be putting it mildly). Elizabeth's room was an adventure unto itself. It reminded me a great deal of my childhood home, stepping over piles of junk in all directions. In my mind I would think that we would have to resort to drastic measures, like perhaps a bulldozer, to even begin to sort it all out. She almost never cleaned her room. It didn't matter how angry I got. It didn't matter how many privileges she lost, or if she would have to face her life grounded until she was twenty-one. Her room was not getting cleaned!

Elizabeth also tended to lie. She was good at it. (So much for my first house rule: "Honesty.") She could tell you an elaborate lie and stick to it no matter what. Even if the lie was going to bring her down, she would go down, lie intact, insisting to the end, that her story was the whole truth, nothing but the truth.

The other side of the coin is that Elizabeth was the most sensitive, warm and generous person I have ever known. She was a great comfort when I was feeling down. She was spirited and soulful, and her spirit was courageous and beautiful. Elizabeth was amazingly artistic, and had a discerning eye for color. She loved animals, and had a passion for horses. All this and so much more.

At the age of fifteen, Elizabeth grew very rebellious. My sweet and sensitive girl became angry, and she aimed her anger toward me in a big way. She began running away from home regularly. Once she ran away with a traveling carnival!

It became clear that she wanted to live with her father. Danny had spent about six months living with Brian previously in his life, and Elizabeth wanted that opportunity, as well. Brian refused her; and then she was really angry. She needed her dad! In my mind, it was good for the kids to actually experience life with their father. Brian and I were opposite ends of the spectrum, and I had hoped that they could take the most out of each lifestyle. Elizabeth's father's refusal set her on the war path.

She did end up living with Brian for a while, but by the time that took place, Elizabeth was angry at him also, and she acted out a lot at his house.

The period of time that my children lived with their father was the first time that I was able to see them and completely enjoy their company as people, without having to ask if their homework was done.

...

And Jill! no lass
Scarce ever has
Made bigger tracks on the country grass;
For her only fun
Was to romp and run,
Bare-headed, bare-footed, in wind and sun.

...

—Clara Doty Bates

14

Retrospect

I had opened my own business at this time, and had enough work to get by. Danny was in the Navy. Elizabeth was living at her dad's. This was the first time in my entire life that I was actually free. It was nice!

I still had no desire to go out much, and often not at all. Except for the times that I spent with my friends, I was content to make myself a good meal and listen to my favorite music in the comfort of my own home. My personal growth had skyrocketed during those years. I felt proud and happy with who I had become.

My relationship with my parents also took many turns. My mother was often out of control. She constantly barged in unexpectedly. No call first, and not even a knock … just the door swinging opened, and there she would be. I worked hard at the "call first" suggestion, but she never got it.

My relationship with my mother never grew past what it was when I was a child. I tried several times to develop a friendship, or form some kind of a bond, but it was impossible; and it was ridiculous!

Conversely, my father recognized my growth and accomplishments. He looked at me with respect and maybe even pride. We never got back to that tender little place that began to develop when I first left home, before the shit hit the fan. But, at this point it didn't matter that much.

He and my mother were still enjoying a periodic fuck. My mother had become jealous of my relationship with him, and would never leave us alone together, fearing that we might talk about her. It was all as bizarre as ever, and I completely ran out of patience for both of their ludicrous antics. I often avoided any opportunity to be around them. I know for sure that I loved my dad deeply. I had hoped that a day might come when I could visit with him and Margaret; although I did not hold my breath.

After a while, my parent's presence in my life had declined significantly. This was particularly true with my father. I don't remember the last time I saw him, but I wish I remembered; because if I had known that I would never see him again, I would have made it a point to carefully preserve his image and words, and tone … in my mind. I would have made a deliberate intensive eye contact that unmistakably told him that I loved him for exactly who he was. Whatever strength, acuity, perseverance, or social skills that I have, I got from him. I can't explain that even to myself, but I know it's true.

My mother moved two states south and retired, and I don't think that she saw my father much, if at all, after that; although she was still living in the tired old fantasy that Dad would "come to his senses," leave Margaret, and come back to her.

As I have stated, I don't have a whole lot of patience. I might not have any at all! So it was difficult for me to tolerate her complete denial of reality. I could not join her in this perverted fantasy life. Curiously, my brother and my mother had established a mutually comfortable space in which to interact. He lived with her on and off through the years. Howard was a full-fledged alcoholic and had been for most of his life. He almost never worked, and when he did, it never lasted for more than a couple of months. But Mom was always there to keep him safe. Howard remained my mother's shining light. His great looks took a beating through the years of reckless living and heavy drinking, but Mom could see none of it. To her, he was perfect in all respects.

Mom's and Howard's years of screaming matches had become well developed, and accepted by both, as part of their daily routine. Howard had acquired many of Mom's quirky traits. Spending time with them was disturbing to me. But in truth, I was glad they had each other, because for sure, they did not have me. I felt as though I was an alien from a different planet, and almost never saw them.

15

Unconditional Love

So now, before I get into what may very well be the most significant adventure of my life, I have a fervent desire to say a word or two about "Unconditional Love."

Over and over, throughout my life, I have heard the words "unconditional love."

The only way those words could ring true to me would be if, and only if, they included a caring bond between people, where there is a mutual respect and concern, "in earnest," for each other's well-being.

Friendship and love should be free. As in: I love you, and it's free. You don't owe me anything because I love you.

If I give you a gift for some reason, it is free. You do not owe me a gift now or at any time in the future.

If I perform a task to help you, it's because I care about you, and it's free. You don't owe me a task.

There is no greater gift in life than a true friendship ... and in a real friendship, there is no tit for tat. There should be no owing. Because then, it is not a friendship; it is a business agreement.

In my mind, this applies to everyone in your life, including family.

No one has the right to expect things, or bully you, or imply that you are a failure as a person who lets them down.

If someone is making demands, or is dishonest, or speaks to you in a disrespectful tone, that person is not your friend.

I don't believe that anyone is obligated to subject himself to the demands of some arbitrary, unwritten, rules under the guise of love or family.

Friendship should be comfortable and healing.

If you are surrounding yourself with people, any people, who are demanding, condescending, or unkind ... life is short ... make an assessment.

And if these people are expecting your complete cooperation by virtue of shared background, or blood ... they should get real!

People who blatantly overstep boundaries in the name of love and friendship are playing a game, and they are in it for themselves.

If you allow a relationship like this to exist in your life, you subject yourself to the exhausting continuous effort of protecting your space, while diplomatically trying to hold them at bay.

If you have to watch your back, that is not a friendship.

Friendship should not require a strategy.

So in my humble opinion, there is no such thing as unconditional love.

Love is conditional upon the presence of respect and acceptance.

*And I am privileged to be able to make the following
statement from the deepest part of my heart:
"Friendship and love do indeed exist!
And they are not unconditional.
They are, however, clear and open and free!"*
—TLC

16

Off to the Country

The pleasures of my life have always been rooted in nature. I love the wind, the smell of grass, the sound of rain, and the beauty and peace that falling snow brings.

I had fantasized about country living for as long as I could remember, and often thought about living on more land, with fewer people around, and less noise. I knew that I could thrive in a rural sparsely-populated country setting. With Danny in the Navy and Elizabeth living with her dad, I was pretty much free to go wherever I wanted. I was thirty-eight years old, and I had a successful business that I deliberately kept small enough to work alone. In the far reaches of my mind, I could almost see the possibility of making this dream happen. But the reality of uprooting myself, selling my house, geographically choosing a place to live, finding a house, and moving the business—all while working every day—seemed insurmountable.

And the thought of leaving my little house that I loved so much—the place where I had grown and discovered myself—was disconcerting to say the least. I had lived in this house for sixteen years. How could I trust that I would ever feel this comfortable, somewhere else? This would be a gamble! So before I even got started, I would have to accept the fact that I could lose part or all of my comfortable, peaceful existence.

Then one day, this thought was set in motion: There were many steps that would need to be taken one by one. All aspects had to be synchronized. Each completed step led to the next. There were lists in my head with the top item being the priority. When the top item got crossed off, the list would automatically move up.

I needed two attorneys: one for here and one for there. I decided to go two states north, which landed me five states away from Mom and Howard.

So I was selling, buying, hiring inspection engineers, driving eight to nine hours round trip, back and forth; and I had to keep the business alive while all this activity was going on.

By the time I was approaching the home stretch, I had broken out in a rash, and my face swelled up with such intensity that my eyes were almost completely closed. This was an unbelievable journey for me—a person who loved sitting in the quiet peaceful embrace of my own living room. But once it began, there was no turning back!

The adventure of my life was in full swing! The process began in late March and concluded in the middle of August.

As soon as I had a firm deal on the house that I was living in, I began packing little by little, disassembling my wonderful home. There were eighty carefully-packed cartons holding all my treasures and stacked in the living room.

I had found a little house in the woods, tucked into the side of a hill, sitting on upwards of three acres of land. The house was just large enough to provide a designated area for business on the ground level, with living quarters on the next floor, and a half loft above the living room. Every single view was charming, natural, and beautiful. The driveway was right off a main highway, but it was long and wound around a bit. So the setting was quiet and private.

I can say without a doubt that when I drove up the driveway for the first time, bells were ringing in my head. I knew before I even entered the house that I could live there. The house itself was not fancy, nor luxurious, but it was sound, and that's what I was going for. It was well engineered from the foundation to the roof. I loved the ambiance inside and outside.

I dealt with the legal aspects of this adventure one by one — getting it all neatly tied up on both ends.

The prospect of leaving my familiar home was not as traumatic as I had imagined, but as time wound down to my last week there, I made a mental note of things that I would miss, and things that I would be okay with leaving. There were wonderful moments and memories there: holiday meals and festivities, gatherings of friends, preparing for winter with the kids in late fall, warm fires on brisk days, and the comforting sound of the oil burner humming on cold winter nights. I loved every moment that I lived there!

But I had noticed as time passed that the backyard looked smaller each year. The neighbors, whom I liked, were too close. The town itself was becoming more densely populated. There was more traffic, and more traffic lights. And two days before I moved out, I woke up to the clanking sound of garbage trucks, noisily collecting trash at the curb. I knew that I could live without that. I would always treasure my time here ... but it was time to move on.

So with a full heart, an open mind, and wild with excitement, at the tender age of thirty-eight, I was off to the country!

I had only been in my new house three times. I wasn't even sure how to get to the exact spot. There were so many questions in my mind. How long would it take to adjust to living there? Would I be comfortable and productive working there? Would I be afraid in the house at night? How would the piano sound?

I pulled slowly into the driveway. The sight of the house and the woods exuded so much warmth that it almost made my heart ache.

The house looked mighty and strong as if to say, "I will keep you safe." The large, stately, aged trees said, "I will protect you from the winter winds." I in turn, scanned the little forest that was now in my charge, and made a silent promise to always respect it. I entered my new home and was drawn in like a magnet. There was no doubt that I belonged there! *Great day in the morning!*

Within two days, I was unpacked, pictures were up, and music was playing. *My God! Was I dreaming?*

Every view out of every window was seductive. I was on a natural high and more excited than I had ever been before. I had to pay close attention to finances. I had to prepare the lower level of the house to accommodate my business, and I needed to begin working as soon as possible.

If I were to describe this entire experience as to how it affected my awareness and how it enriched my insight, I would liken it to hammering a nail into a tree, leaving the nail head out about one quarter of an inch. Over the years, as the tree grew, it would begin to reach the nail head and eventually cover the edges, leaving only the flat shiny surface of the nail head exposed. If the nail were a person, as the tree grew, the person would slowly, without realizing it lose peripheral vision; and after a while, only be able to see straight ahead. After I moved, I felt as though I was dislodged and re-positioned, thereby restoring complete and renewed peripheral vision that I didn't even know I had lost.

I'm going to say something now, and I say it clearly and unequivocally: After living in this house and on this property for some thirty plus years, the beauty, comfort and charm is reaffirmed each day, every single time I look out a window. And more than that, I haven't taken one glorious moment for granted. I am still in awe of the magnificent sunsets that I am privileged to witness from the comfort of my favorite chair in my humble home.

I got completely settled into my home in weeks. I had two rooms built on the ground level for business, and was back to work. Business was good, perhaps too good, because I was working way more hours than I would have liked. But the joy of living in the house was so energizing that it was hard to be anything but ecstatic all day, every day. My goal was to maintain the house, take care of the grounds, and pay off the mortgage as soon as I could. So I proceeded to work hard and put all of my earnings into the house and mortgage.

I did not crave vacations or fancy clothes. Home was my favorite place to be whether I was working or not.

I was hoping my father would call. I hadn't spoken to him since way before the move — way before I had even thought to move. I was anxious to tell him about the house and property, and about business. I knew that he would appreciate my lifestyle and my success. I had visions of having Dad and Margaret visiting. I would meet her in my home, and Dad would be proud! But years had passed, and I hadn't heard from him.

I knew that he called my mother once in a while, and to be honest it annoyed me because I was sure that she would never encourage him to contact me.

17

Dad

One October day, my mother called and said, "I hate to tell you this … I think your father died!" Only my mother could "think" someone died. And besides being devastated, I despised the very idea that it was she who was giving me this news.

I asked, "Why do you 'think' that?"

"Well because I haven't heard from him in months, and then I was reading a list of names in a newspaper, and his name was on it … and it said 'may they rest in peace'!"

I can't even describe how I felt. I was flushed and sick. Dad, the only parent I had with a brain, was gone!

And then Mom said, "It looks like he died three months ago!"

Well, now I was enraged! Three months, and I wasn't contacted … and why wasn't I contacted? Because my simple-minded, revenge-seeking, asshole of a mother played her sick little game that prevented me from having a normal relationship with my father. I wanted to strangle her! I wanted to call her cruel and hurtful names. I wanted to tell her that she was a fucking whore who never had an ounce of dignity.

The fact is … that she would not have heard or owned any of it. Mom truly believed that she was justified in every decision that she made. That there was nothing wrong with my childhood or her strange relationship with my father.

Then she asked, in a feeble little voice, "Does this mean I'm a widow?"

At that moment, I detested her!

After that, I saw my mother maybe, four or five times, and each time I came home doubting my sanity. If she called me, I made it short and sweet, and after caller ID came along, I never answered the phone if I saw her number come up.

My grief over my father's death was so intense. I wanted to call Margaret and embrace her and cry, but I didn't. I had grandiose thoughts of visiting her, telling her that I didn't belong to the sick dysfunctional duo of Mom and Howard, and that I wish she could have been my mother … but Dad was gone! What would have been the point? And if I met and talked with her, information would have been revealed that would have ultimately hurt her. It was a horrible set of circumstances.

There was no saving grace for me. I simply had to accept that Dad no longer existed. There would be no one and no place where I could find solace in regard to Dad's death. I located the cemetery where he was buried, and I got in the car, drove in, and sat by his grave for hours … Thank God, I had this wonderful home to return to!

As I grieved for my father, I thought about what I had accomplished since the last time we sat across the table from each other, until the time I learned of his death. I had come so far! And always present in my mind was the anticipation of our next visit and the revelations I would share with him: about my gutsy relocation; about how successful and well reputed my business was; and how well I was able to manage money. These were all things that would have impressed him. Finally, I could make him proud!

I often thought of myself in terms of greatness. If I could have patted myself on the back, I would have! If I would have commented to myself, I might have said. "Good Job!" or "Well Done!"

But now that Dad was gone, being great was not as much fun.

. . .

Ah, when to the heart of man
Was it ever less than a treason
To go with the drift of things,
To yield with a grace to reason,
And bow and accept the end
Of a love or a season?
— Robert Frost

18

My Children

Soon after I came to terms with saying goodbye to my father, Elizabeth decided to go to Texas. In those days, it was trendy to go somewhere to find yourself. Elizabeth didn't know anyone in Texas, but a friend of hers was going, and Elizabeth decided to go along.

She would call periodically and tell me all the things she thought I wanted to hear. She said that she was in school taking art courses, and needed money for books. Just to prove that this was true, Elizabeth offered to send me an official copy of her grades. I requested that she please have it notarized!

Elizabeth's spirit soared! I often marveled at the exuberance that she applied to everything in her life and became exhausted just listening to her.

I don't think that I have ever been flexible. I think I was born set in my ways. I don't like crowds. I don't like noise. My lifestyle is healthy. I tend to be a bit reclusive. I'm fine with all of that; but what I'm saying is that I was this way all my life, including when I was raising the kids.

Both Danny and Elizabeth, in my opinion, had lifestyles that were a bit noisy. I am happy to report that they both were flexible, and could go with the flow. The only flow that I could ever go with was my own! I am sincerely pleased that my subdued lifestyle did not inhibit the boisterous side of their personalities. They both were open to crowds, fun, and noise! This is not in any way, a criticism … just an observation.

Since I made my big move. Danny, Elizabeth, and I connected mainly on the phone. I spoke to both of them often, sometimes every day, and my conversations with Elizabeth might last hours and include vigorous laughing jags. I didn't see a lot of them. And I rarely saw them together, but I am as much to blame for that as they.

I was completely tied up in work. My work owned me! It dictated when, if ever, I would have a free weekend or holiday. It dictated how much sleep I got. It pretty much ran my life. But it was a necessary evil and a responsibility that I took seriously. I wasn't happy that it swallowed up my time, but I loved the work. And except for the heavy schedule, it was on my own terms. There was no driving in traffic, and no nine to five. It was my own vehicle. And it was paying for my home!

So Danny and Elizabeth were out in the world! I did not miss them. They were in my thoughts all the time, and I certainly loved them, but I was at last living and enjoying my own life for the very first time.

I wished that they lived more cautiously. Danny was headstrong, and Elizabeth was from my standpoint, a little too wild. But they were young and testing their wings. I had never experienced my youth in a normal fashion, so

I assumed and hoped that both of them were on a normal course of life. I tried not to allow myself to worry, although it was tempting, because it seemed a useless drain of energy.

The three of us had lived in a home where music reigned and served as a religion, as well as a philosophy. I was still living with the truths of so many songwriters and poets, and I hoped that my children had retained and applied some of those profound messages into their daily comings and goings.

> *You are the bows from which your children*
> *As living arrows are sent forth.*
> *The archer sees the mark upon the path of the infinite,*
> *And He bends you with His might*
> *That His arrows may go swift and far,*
> *Let your bending in the archer's hand be for gladness;*
> *For even as He loved the arrow that flies,*
> *So he loves also the bow that is stable.*
> — Khalil Gibran

The next mind-boggling event took place early one morning when the phone rang just after midnight. It was a hospital in Dallas calling to tell me that Elizabeth had been in a serious accident. She was a passenger in a truck that had gone off the road and dropped forty feet. She was severely injured. I did not get all the details, except that she was stable for the moment, and that her condition could turn either way. I tried to remain as calm as possible, and think clearly. I called her brother and her father, and I got on a plane.

Flying to DFW Airport, I could not contain the thoughts of the moment when I first held her … and the adorable little girl she grew into ... how she ran away from home with the carnival ... her historically unkempt room.

Arriving at the hospital, I found that my son had gotten there before me. This was a comfort, and made me proud.

The list of Elizabeth's injuries was overwhelming. Her back was broken, along with a clean break in her femur. Her nose was broken, and she had lost several teeth. When I got to her, they had just finished suturing her lip back together.

Fortunately, her thinking processes were clear and coherent, and her prognosis was better than expected. She had a steel rod inserted into her broken leg. She needed to be in a body cast for months. Then after all the swelling was down, and she was ambulatory, we could address her dental issues. Elizabeth had a roommate who seemed confident enough to be able to provide care for her when she left the hospital.

Although this was a horrifying event, Elizabeth would fully recover. Elizabeth was a stunningly beautiful young woman, and quite vain. Her appearance took a real hit, and her body would forever ache in the damp and cold weather and would never be quite as flexible as before.

Amazingly though, six months later, she attended a formal affair in spike heels, bouncing around like a butterfly, and looking as beautiful as ever. Her vibrant indomitable spirit amazed me time after time.

Unfortunately the pain medication did indeed create an addiction. This was a constant underlying source of deep concern for me. My relationship with Elizabeth from that point went back and forth from high to low.

Elizabeth loved motorcycles and dated bikers. If I dwelled on the thought of her sitting on the back of a motorcycle, riding long distances from state to state, with her already injured back, it would make me crazy.

The plain truth is that I could not control Elizabeth's life! Also, from time to time, she would display personality changes due to the prescription meds that she denied taking, but that I knew she was taking. I could not contain my frustration with her behavior and denial, and this resulted in long spans of not talking or communicating with each other.

When she visited, it would either be good, or intensely bad. There were times, during a visit that she would come into my room and talk all night, pouring her heart out. Her drug dependence had taken a toll. I could see it. She had lost many opportunities because of it. Elizabeth never blamed her problems on anyone. She would say to me many times, "Mom, I did this to myself!" I always respected her for being able to take responsibility for her own behavior.

I begged her to go into rehab. I said "Go for as long as it takes, and I will visit every day," but that never happened. The pattern of back and forth, up and down, continued for years. She got married, and then divorced.

Although Elizabeth and I were friends, as a mother I could not find in her the little girl with the shining eyes that I once knew.

Danny was now married, and living in the midwest. His marriage for the most part was unremarkable. On the plus side, he had a great work ethic. He was a good provider, he kept his home in good repair, and had his father's talent for landscape. He provided me with three grandsons, and on all three occasions I felt blessed!

Unfortunately, Danny and I were still butting heads. To me, it seemed as though he felt that by virtue of his birth, I owed him bailouts of one kind or another for the rest of his life. It was like a continual tug of war. He would still take pot shots at me, but as before, just enough to jab a little, but not enough to have to acknowledge his discontent. Once in a while I enjoyed his company, but more often than not, it was stressful.

As I have stated previously, I will not tolerate friction in my life. And I will not step into the arena with anyone for any reason. I will not argue or defend myself about anything to anyone.

And all are free to interpret that however they will!

19

Observing Life

It seems like I have spent a good deal of time over the years watching people interact. As I realized my own emotional growth, I became interested in how people evolve and connect with one another.

The circumstances of our lives, in all probability over the years, twist our psyches. And although we can't control many of these circumstances, we can choose to either be victimized, or gain awareness and strength from them.

Being a very private person, I do not expose my vulnerable side to anyone whom I don't completely trust. And that trust is a rare find! I live in my vulnerable element as much as possible. It is the softest part of me. It is the element that most defines my personal freedom. And it is the part of me that I give to my friends. How great it is to feel comfortable, free and completely accepted by friends who know and love me!

During the course of a lifetime, when meeting and dealing with people, it doesn't take long to measure the proximity of one psyche to another. If there is any depth at all between the people involved, this assessment of distance happens automatically.

A person can be a fine person—a really good person—but if the distance is vast, communication is limited. In that case, exposing a vulnerability would be undesirable, and serve no purpose. But, sometimes in life, through business of one kind or another, an interaction is required. Then the best move would be to take care of the business at hand in a personable, upstanding, responsible and civilized manner, and then move on.

If the distance is short, and in sync, then true, enjoyable, and satisfying communication is possible, along with the potential for a friendship. This is way less common (for me anyway).

Sometimes the distance is short, but not in sync. Herein lies the most uncomfortable circumstance for me: This would be where friction, stress, and conflict lurk. People can see you, and they are remarkably friendly, but they don't actually like you. They want to control you for whatever reason (and often the reason is jealously). They want to be close to you, and lean on you because of your individuality, or your strength, and high standards. You would think that this would be simple to recognize and avoid. But it is not so black and white. It does, however, eventually become crystal clear.

If the latter is the case, I would say to anyone, "Run for the hills as soon as possible, and don't look back!" It is not your job to stroke an ego or be an example of virtue to those who have none. It is not your job to be nice to everyone just because you are a nice person. Save it for those who are sincere.

In my younger days, when I first became aware of life, I did not always trust my instincts with backhanded people, thereby prolonging the inevitable, until an uncomfortable situation became unbearable. How much time and energy did I waste? As I grew older, I realized with each passing year that time is at a premium. Now, I just cut to the chase. If you are feeling a discord with someone, listen to your gut. Life is short. Get in the wind!

The simple, but powerful truth is that "people don't change." No one needs someone with an underlying resentment towards them in his life. And people who prey on others live in denial and don't see themselves. Even if they did, they would never own their bad behavior.

As I see it, my goal for my life is to be as strong and true as I can be to myself ... to live the best life possible ... to tap into my creative cache to the max, while caring for the people and beliefs that I treasure.

A small-minded person who thinks quite highly of himself, once asked me in an accusatory tone, "Oh, so it's all about you?"

I wouldn't even waste my time responding to someone so narrow, but here and now ... let's look at that question. Who should my life be about? Should my soul and my days be about other people? Even when the truest of love exists, each individual's life is about himself. I think it is called self-respect.

A desire to be supportive to the people and the principals you care about always exists. But it is not a duty!

It is a duty to always see the truth.

It is a duty to keep oneself healthy and happy in mind and body.

It is a duty to never intentionally be unkind to anyone (unless it is driven by self defense).

It is a duty to always keep your word.

The only duty applicable to people other than yourself would be the duty of parents, to demonstrate to young children, as best they can, the difference between right and wrong.

And here is an interesting question to ponder, relevant to this subject:

Where do you draw the line between honesty and selfishness?

I am not bound to please thee with my answers.
—William Shakespeare

20

Mid Life, but No Crisis

As my life continued on, I woke up one day and found myself approaching the age of fifty! Oh my God! I remember thinking that it was just about all over. How funny is that?

Right around this crisis period, Leonard Cohen released a new album.

He addressed life and death in his usual manner, except in this new material, the confrontation of his own experience with aging, acquired wisdom, and the strength to embrace life as it happens, seemed a little more potent. Sometimes, something comes along that just hits the spot. His words seamlessly carved their way into my soul and gave me the courage to go ahead and be exactly who I was. Age did not matter … life mattered.

I was better at fifty than I had ever been in my life, and Leonard Cohen's words gave me the courage and grace to live it. Verse after verse, erasing any vulnerability that might have weaseled its way into my psyche. I never tried to hide or mask my age in any way, and this gave me an amazing capacity for balance and personal freedom.

I never got a handle on my schedule at work. And I rarely had time off. I was becoming concerned about the possibility of ever being able to retire. Everything that I earned over the years had gone into the house. I had replaced most of the windows and the roof, and addressed all other maintenance issues as they surfaced. I had fine-tuned the inside of the house to fit my needs exactly, and I knew and loved every inch of my home. The property required periodic tree servicing. I took care of everything as it was needed. I had come to know the people in the area, and felt like a fixture there. And it felt good!

At age fifty-one, I brought home a golden retriever puppy; she was a joy. Three years later, I brought in a yellow Labrador retriever, and he also was beyond delightful. So two years after that ... another yellow lab! The three dogs added love, spice, and healthy activity to my life. I cherished them all. They would patiently sit by my side as I was bogged down with work. There were days when I would work twelve-to-sixteen hours, and finish up at four in the morning. Often, on those mornings, I would sit up until first light, then drive a couple of miles to a local hiking trail, and off we would all go! Watching the dogs run and play on those hikes was delightful!

I dated once in a while, and I did have a couple of short "flings." But mostly I worked, and I was fine with that. I guess the bottom line was that my business was a tremendous source of pride and satisfaction for me. Over the years, I had turned down opportunities to make more money, which might have meant a structured schedule, and more time off ... but it also would mean less control and integrity in the work. There was no question in my mind that I was doing what I wanted to do, the way I wanted to do it!

I had no contact at all with my ex-husband once the kids were grown. He had said some unkind things to Danny and Elizabeth about me over the years. But that was no surprise, and really ... who cared?

Brian's third wife, Bridgett, the one after me, had died, and apparently Brian was dating vigorously. So after a year or so, he was getting married again to wife #4. In all honesty, I wished him the best.

One day he called and said, "Hi, I'm in the process of getting a marriage license, and I need some information from our divorce papers." I stopped what I was doing, went to the file cabinet, got the information he needed, and provided it cheerfully. Then I sincerely wished him the very best of luck.

My energy toward Brian was completely neutral. I didn't like him, or not like him. And so, Brian had a grand wedding once again.

Years flew by, and my early sixties closed in swiftly. I had pretty much come to terms with life, and other than my ongoing heavy work schedule and serious concern for a financially-stable retirement, I was essentially content, and still as grateful as ever that I had made my move up to the country so many years before. I still felt privileged to be living my life in such a peaceful setting.

People don't just land somewhere. Life is rarely the luck of the draw. Life is exactly what you make it. Being true to who you are is not simply a virtue that you can conveniently take or leave. It is not always easy to be true to yourself, but it is always, most definitely crucial.

21

Mom

The last time I communicated with my mother, she was alone and dealing with the limitations of age. Howard was off somewhere in his luxury car, spending the last of her money. Mom still talked to me like I was second-hand goods that existed only to be used. She knew from previous contact with me that I was out of the game, but she never stopped trying to tangle me up in her useless corrupt values and fantasies. I had no regrets about my disassociation with her.

What did I learn from Mom?

I learned that you can't change people. And if they are blind, you can't make them see who you are!

Somewhere in this time period, I became interested in my ancestry. One day, while I was sitting at the computer with five extra minutes on my hands, I typed in a couple of names … then with no warning, there it was! Mom's obituary!

I generally don't have a problem with words, but I have to say that I am running out of ways to describe the shock and continual affirmation that I was never a part of any family!

Mom's obituary stated that she had a son. Yes, that's right. That was the whole story … just a son!

For a moment I had questions. Where was Howard? What were the circumstances? I could have called, but for what? This was a simple confirmation of something that I had always known.

I was not devastated, and I did not cry. I knew that death had gravity, and I felt that. I was not angry, nor resentful.

And so I added one more fucked-up development to my ever-growing list.

22

Howard

I almost never saw my brother. We talked maybe once every few years. Howard's life always puzzled me, because he simply allowed himself to stagnate. My mother had showered him with all the unnecessary luxuries that he craved until she ran out of money. Howard never experienced the satisfaction of working towards something and then achieving it. I thought that was sad.

But it wasn't sad to him! I never heard him say the words, "I wish I had," or "I should have." So who was I to say those words about him? Who was I to criticize?

Howard had savvy. He had insight. I knew this just from the handful of solid conversations that we had over the years. Once in a while, Howard would make a statement that was so simple, and yet so profound, such as: "In life we all have exactly what we want."

I never heard from my brother after Mom died. And now that she was gone, I wondered where he lived and how he was surviving. This was not by any means a concern, as much as a curiosity.

As I moved along on my own journey, I was becoming increasingly aware that I was tired. I was okay for the moment, but I didn't know how I would get along if I ever stopped working. I thought about this often, as I had not saved enough money to supplement my social security checks for an appreciable amount of time. How long would I last with no income? That was the big question! This was becoming a reality that I would ultimately have to face.

On the other hand, the thought of not working sounded more and more appealing with each passing day. I did not have extravagant desires for luxury of any nature. Just being able to provide for my basic daily needs would do the trick. I figured that the inevitable would eventually happen, and the chips would fall however they would fall.

Two years after my mother died, I got a call from my nephew (my brother's son), in California. Howard had died one month before his sixty-fifth birthday. The information I got was pieced together because no one had seen or heard from him in years. For the most part, he was homeless. Howard had somehow managed to hold on to his car. So what this means is that he was homeless, living in a Jaguar. He had been spotted in a park in our old neighborhood.

Apparently, his many years of drinking had caused a thinning of the walls of his esophagus, and he ultimately bled to death. He lay in the morgue for a month because no one knew who he was. It was by chance that they located Howard's son. It had been intended by the state to bury Howard in a mass grave, but my nephew arranged to have him cremated and transported to the cemetery where my mother was. And Howard is there in an urn, next to my mother's urn. It's almost poetic!

My brother's death, along with his life, saddened me greatly. It was sobering, and exasperating! I have never visited their graves, and can't imagine that I ever will.

And so, I am the last of the four. But no more alone than I have ever been.

23

As Time Passed

From time to time, my son, Danny, would offer his services to me for various repairs and heavy tasks around the house …. "for a fee." But that was okay. I had accepted those conditions, and except for once, Danny was paid for several of these projects. His requested fees, by the way, were exorbitant, and I could have hired someone local for way less money. But I was agreeable to our arrangement. We got to see each other, and he usually did a good job. So he would come over for a day or two, and work around the house. Routinely, after I paid him Danny would whine about the price of gas, so I would fill his gas tank also.

If Elizabeth came up to work, she did not want money, but I insisted that she take pay … because if I was paying one, then I would pay the other.

The demand for money from Danny was always present. If I called him on it, he would deny it completely. As annoying as this was, I was quite used to it.

One year Danny was making plans to visit me with my youngest grandson. Danny was planning to do a little work in the kitchen while they were here. I did not have the time to buy the supplies needed, and was honestly not up for the mess and disruption, so I suggested that he just come over and visit. I hadn't seen my grandson in a while and was looking forward to catching up.

When I suggested this to Danny, he became angry. I'm still not sure exactly why. But Danny then informed me that he would be needing money for gas both ways. I was becoming extremely put off, but I said okay. The amount of money that he wanted for gas was completely insane, and this now became an insult to my intelligence. So I said ... "You know what, don't come!"

This caused a rift between us that would not be easily reversed. But ... I was no longer willing to buy Danny's acceptance and love! And he was not willing at all ... to take the pole out of his whiny little ass!

After more than twenty years in this house, I decided to put a small bathroom in the loft by my bedroom. This was huge for me. I was beyond excited. It would be called a closet bathroom in the world of carpenters and plumbers. I dreaded the intrusion of workers, and the mess that went with it, but I was ready to bite the bullet so that I could finally enjoy the convenience.

Upon completion, it was an absolute joy. I was too busy to take the time to paint it; and to be honest, as long as the toilet flushed and there was running water in the sink, I did not care in the least about the walls. Even after more than two years passed, I would from time to time have fleeting moments thinking how nice it would look finished. But still, I was not willing to give up a rare day off to paint it.

Elizabeth had been in a great frame of mind for an extended period of time, and would call for very long chats, more often than usual. She sounded better than ever. She was working hard and consistently at beating down her demons. She had been involved in a rehab program for over a year, and was attending workshops, seeing a doctor once a month, and having blood work done regularly as they tried to wean her off her dependence to prescription meds.

This seemed different from other times. She wanted to come up for a visit and paint the little bathroom. She kept saying, "I really want to get that done for you." I took note of that because there was almost an urgency in her voice.

So we set up a time period, with dates for this visit. I had about a month to work my schedule, so that I could free up a few days to spend some time with her. She called every day and talked about her anticipation of our visit.

We discussed meals and desserts. Elizabeth requested meatloaf and mashed potatoes for one night, and we planned to bake a fresh blueberry pie for dessert.

She would call and say, "Mom, only thirteen days, and I'll be there!" The next day she'd say, "Only twelve days!" Each day she would count down. I was becoming as excited as Elizabeth. I had no expectations in any way. It felt like we were going to just really enjoy each other, and anything that got done would be fine.

When I food shopped, I looked for all of her favorite foods. I planned out special breakfasts, as well as dinners. Blueberries were not in season, and I remember spending over thirty dollars to get enough blueberries for one pie. We hadn't seen each other in a long while, and I didn't care how much the blueberries cost.

I barely finished up work in time, but come what may, I was taking the time off!

24

A State of Grace

This didn't feel like an ordinary visit. It felt very special. I don't know why. I picked Elizabeth up on a Wednesday night. She had taken the ferry across the sound. It was early spring, and spring was in the air. When we found each other by the dock, it was about as good as it gets. I grabbed hold of her and held her. I remember vividly feeling the softness of her brown suede jacket and the smell of her hair. She was so happy that she sparkled.

As soon as we got in the car, we began laughing. Everything was funny! We laughed all the way back to my house, a ninety-minute drive. I had baked a sweet bread earlier, and when we got back home, we had some bread and tea, and talked for hours.

The next day we were off to Home Depot, and chose the paint and brushes, and rollers. In an effort to save time, we were running up and down the store aisles. It began to resemble a comedy, and soon we were out of control laughing again. We laughed through a Taco Bell lunch, and then laughed all the way home.

Elizabeth jumped right into action, taping the bathroom. She had the primer coat on that day. I cooked and baked; and in between kitchen activity, I went upstairs and kept her company. I had noticed that she had her nails done in purple. She was scraping some dried paint with her nails, and I offered her some plastic gloves. She said no, that her nails would be fine.

Later, we had our meatloaf dinner. It was good, and the conversation was positive and interesting and lasted for hours. I felt closer and more connected to her during that visit than ever before … ever in her whole life! It was like we had entered into a different dimension, and we were dancing in a perfect rhythm.

Those few days, we talked about life's experiences and lessons learned: about her life, her hopes, her childhood … and about my own journey. There was not one single negative moment, and there was complete acceptance on both ends. Elizabeth seemed to have a confidence and wisdom that I had never seen in her before. I remember feeling so grateful that she would now, finally, make it to the finish line … And in her face, and in her eyes and expression, I could clearly see my little girl.

Whatever state of grace we were in, it was a phenomenon. And I hoped that we had reached and could remain in a lasting common ground. This was the most gratifying and relevant experience that I have ever had as a parent.

It was a week or so before Mother's Day, and Elizabeth brought with her, a gift for me, of butterflies under glass. She had picked out the colors specifically to match the freshly-painted bathroom. After the bathroom was finished and reassembled, I hung the picture. It was the icing on the cake!

Elizabeth had no access to email, or social media. Her computer was barely alive. As a gesture of thanks, I had ordered her a new computer and camera. The boxes had arrived the week before and were waiting for her when she got here. We spent some time setting up the computer, and she walked around the house and property taking scenic videos while narrating them in the process. We transferred the files from the camera into her new computer. She created a folder and named it "Visit at Mom's." It contained the videos and still shots of her time spent here, including the bathroom, the dogs, and the blueberry pie!

This profound event that we were experiencing together was so filled with love and so absolute, and was happening in the softest vein imaginable. I was entirely aware that in those few days, Elizabeth and I had somehow traveled light-years together.

She had turned her life around. I couldn't have been more proud! At one point, I saw such an elegance about her and said, "Elizabeth, you are so beautiful!" The night before she left, I knew that having her in my life would be more of a comfort and joy than ever before. I would be sad to see her go, but I was ready to get back to work, and she had her own commitments to get home to.

We loaded up the car, and we were off to the ferry the next afternoon. An hour into the drive, Elizabeth realized that she had forgotten her jacket. It was still on a hook in my kitchen where she had hung it the night that she arrived. "Don't worry," I said, "I'll pack it up and UPS it to you tomorrow." Oddly, she said, "no don't, I won't be needing it."

The afternoon was beautiful! The sunshine was dazzling! And we were still laughing at everything! It was not unusual for me to hug Elizabeth to and from visits. But that day, I hugged her tight and long. I said, "I love you. I had such a good time, and I can't wait to see you again." We were standing about three hundred feet from the dock, and I stood there and watched her walk toward the ramp and make her way onto the ferry.

I was truly sad to see her go, but I was distracted immediately from feeling blue by the vivid and surreal events of the past few days. What an incredible time, and oh my God, I have a finished bathroom!

Elizabeth's boyfriend picked her up on the other end. When I got back home, I thought about calling her just to say I had a great time. And then the phone rang, and it was she, calling just to say that she had a great time. We both started laughing!

25

Losing Elizabeth

When I returned to work, I was energized and unstoppable. The thought that stayed with me the most was: *My God, Elizabeth is really going to be okay! Thank you ... Thank you ... Thank you!*

I worked that whole week as though I had just discovered ambition, drive and enthusiasm.

That Thursday, four days after our visit, I was on my way down to work, and as I passed the phone, I picked it up and called Elizabeth.

She sounded so good!

"Oh hi, Mom. I'm just walking out the door. Can I call you back?"

I said, "No, you don't have to. I was thinking about you and just called to say a quick hello ... have a great day."

She replied, "Okay, you too."

I said, "I love you," and hung up and went to work.

I had deadlines that day at work, and I knew I would be working into the next day. But I was totally fine with that. By the time I finished up and got to bed, it was three o'clock Friday morning.

The phone began to ring two hours later at five o'clock. I had just gotten to sleep, and I didn't answer it. It rang again. Now I was fully aware that someone wanted to get through. I didn't answer it. Then my cell phone rang, and I was beginning to feel anxious. Then the land line rang again. I picked it up. "Hello."

I heard Elizabeth's boyfriend on the other end, and he was crying. I obviously knew that whatever happened was very serious, and I almost didn't want to know anymore. Thoughts began racing through my head, inventing scenarios that could be resolved. Maybe there was an accident, and she was hurt. Maybe she's in a coma, but we've done this before; she could still be okay! I reluctantly asked, "What's wrong?"

Through his sobs, he said, "I'm so sorry. Elizabeth passed away last night in her sleep."

I stayed on the line just long enough to try to comprehend this bizarre conversation, but I absolutely did not want to hear anything more, because there was no fucking way I was believing this outrageous news. I was getting right back under the covers and making believe, as hard as I could, that this preposterous phone call had never taken place.

I felt so cold, and I started to shake violently. I began to feel Elizabeth's energy in my brain, crying out to me, "Mommy, I'm afraid!" I thought, *please, please let me wake up from this dreadful nightmare. Oh God, this can't really be happening!*

The phone kept ringing. It was the people in the morgue, wanting me to record a statement releasing Elizabeth's organs. Nothing made any sense! She wasn't even really dead (not in my mind, anyway), and they're asking me for her organs!

In all of my life, with all of my wisdom, and all of my thoughts, and all of my experience, through all of my years — there was no way I was, or could ever have been prepared to know what to do, what to think, or how to ever get through even the next day, let alone this entire ordeal.

I thought of getting into the car and driving to the hospital (which was the hospital where she was born). I would run into the morgue and grab a hold of her hand, and say, "C'mon Elizabeth, let's get out of here now, before this becomes true."

I was as lost as anyone could ever be!

I called my son, who wasn't talking to me, and left a message. "Danny, it's Mom. Call me now! This is an emergency!" … No call back.

I called him again … "Please call me back. This is an EMERGENCY! … No call back.

I thought to myself, *You little fuck, this is an emergency. Being angry doesn't count now. We could be angry later, but right now … this is as bad as it could possible be!*

I stopped calling him, and his failure to respond is anchored in my brain. It is something that I will never forget. Danny called me at two o'clock that afternoon. By then, talking to him didn't matter anymore. It never mattered again after that. The bond of trust that I assumed had existed between us was damaged forever.

My friends stood in close. They were wonderful. But there were no words that could possibly bring relief. Every time the phone rang, my first thought was that it was Elizabeth, followed by an immediate devastating crash into reality.

I went outside and sat in the yard. I couldn't understand anything. Just five days ago, I was watching her laughing in this exact spot. She was alive and sitting right here … last weekend. Oh God, last Saturday when she was here, it was the last Saturday of her life. She would be dead in less than a week.

I looked over at the shed. Elizabeth had painted the shed four years before. She gave it three coats of paint and never spilled a drop. Then, when she was cleaning up, she accidentally stepped in the roller tray full of paint, and stepped on the wooden ramp of the shed, leaving a footprint.

She said, "Oh, I'm sorry!"

I replied, "Don't clean it up. I love it!" And each time I passed in or out of the shed, there would be Elizabeth's perfect footprint.

As I remembered that, I got up and raced over to the ramp of the shed. I thought, *I'll coat it with polyurethane to preserve it forever*. But … it was gone! The rain and snow over the years had worn it away.

I needed someone strong to hold me. I needed to hear someone say, "I'll take care of everything. It will be okay after a while."

I needed to, for once, not have to make the difficult and responsible decisions, and not to have to watch my back!

I would never see her face again and never hear her voice!

I called her father and said, "I don't think I can do this. I don't think I have the stamina to make the arrangements that need to be made." I asked him to please take care of the funeral details. I asked him to please not include a viewing, because she would not have wanted that. Please just arrange for a cremation.

Brian was crying, but through his tears, he mentioned some money that she had received from her past accident and a piece of art work that had value, and a possible will. These were his comments, through his sorrow, on the day of his daughter's death!

Astonished at his tearful statement, I was questioning my own sense of reason and ability to hear. I wanted to shout, "Who the hell gives a shit about that? ... Elizabeth is dead!"

Brian, once again the forever follower, gave the authoritative power over to Elizabeth's boyfriend, who was adamant about having a viewing. When I got the news, I began to cry. My daughter would have hated this! I should have taken care of this myself. And to make matters worse, I would have to be in a room with my child lying in a casket. A child that just last week, was in my home talking and laughing.

Well, I'm not going," I thought. *I can't go. I can't make my way through this!*

I could feel Elizabeth's energy inside of me all that day, and it didn't feel good. It felt as though she was confused, disoriented, and afraid ... but just out of my reach to console her. At one point in the afternoon, I heard and felt a heavy thud; all three dogs jumped, and the hair rose on their backs. I looked around, but no one was here. I was absolutely sure that it was Elizabeth. Her energy had somehow made its way back to me. I could feel her, but not within the reach of my limited scope.

I put the tea kettle on for tea and got a glance of her brown suede jacket still hanging on the hook by the kitchen door where she left it. I went over and embraced it and felt the familiar softness that I had felt just the week before when she was wearing it. And I could smell the scent of her hair. I felt weak and sick, and terribly confused.

Elizabeth's service was about five hours away from my house. I knew that I would not be able to live with myself if I didn't go. I had to go! A great friend, who knew that my only thoughts were ultimately about seeing this through with the most dignity and respect for Elizabeth, and who understood fully that I was barely able to function, suggested that I order yellow roses. And that's what I did. I sent forty-three yellow roses to the funeral parlor (one for each year of her life) with a note that said "I love you ... Mom."

I spoke to Elizabeth's boyfriend, and expressed my disappointment about the viewing. Apparently, this was something that he needed. At this point, there was nothing I could do about it. Brian had signed the papers. People responded to my hesitation about being in a room with my child lying in repose by saying, "Well, you don't have to go over and look at her." But let's get real. Staying away from her would have been impossible, and I knew it. I would have to somehow get through the day.

I entered the room and was drawn to her immediately. The first thing that caught my eye was her purple nails. My heart collapsed ... Elizabeth looked terrible, as if whoever had prepared her was in a hurry. Her beautiful hair, that she took so much pride in, was halfheartedly combed. She would have been mortified, and I felt as though I had let her down. I wanted to sob and beg her forgiveness for allowing this thoughtless exploitation. I wanted to wake up, and shake free, and say, "Thank God, this was just a horrific nightmare."

My ex-husband and wife #4, asked me three times in four hours for money to pay "my share" of the expenses.

The service was filled to capacity with Elizabeth's friends, and I was heartened to see this huge gathering of such diverse people, with one thing in common, "Elizabeth." There were lawyers, history teachers, hairdressers, and bikers, all heartbroken ... all celebrating her.

I stepped outside for a moment, and two bikers on big Harley Davidson motorcycles were revving their engines, getting ready to leave the parking lot. Elizabeth would have loved it, and I was filled with joy for a moment, thinking that the sound of those bikes could not have been more perfect. Her service was filled with all the people whom she loved.

All of her friends singled me out and talked about her kind, sensitive and generous spirit. Meeting this group of people, and listening to the warmth and love that they shared with her, made me grateful that I had attended.

Elizabeth's boyfriend had eluded to a beach party that he was planning, at which time he intended to throw her ashes into the ocean. Elizabeth hated the ocean! I asked him, "Please don't do that!" He made light of my request, and said that it will be great, and that I should come. Upon processing this in my head, I decided that he could not have her remains.

I had sent a check to Brian for the amount that he requested, but it seemed that because Brian had signed for the service, I had no right to her remains. And Brian was releasing them to the boyfriend.

I called my ex-husband, several times, but he did not answer the phone, so I left a message each time saying that I wanted Elizabeth's remains. He did not return any of my calls. (Why was I surprised?) With no response from Brian,

I was on the verge of hysteria and panic. I could not bear the thought of my child's remains being tossed into the ocean during a raucous party with beer cans and cigarette butts. The funeral director adamantly refused my request without an okay from Brian.

I called Brian one more time and left a final message: "In my wildest dreams, under any circumstances, I could never have done this to you. And you don't even have the balls to call me back! Have it your way, Brian. I stopped the check that I sent you."

Miraculously, thirty seconds later, Brian called. "I just walked in the door," he said. "I'll call the funeral director right now, and you can take Elizabeth's remains ... oh, and what about the check?"

Brian's voice and his words were repulsive to me, and I was filled with disgust at the thought of him. I replied, "when the funeral director hands me her ashes, and I get back home and catch my breath ... then I'll re-issue a check!"

One of Elizabeth's greatest passions was horses. She studied them, sketched them, and worked with them. My thoughts were to hold tight for a while and try to assess what had taken place in my life, try to accept my loss, try to grieve; and after some time passed, scatter Elizabeth's remains in some location where wild horses still roamed and played.

My immediate plan, though, was to try to figure out how to be whole without my daughter in the world.

I see you in a fluttering butterfly,
and in the dance of a spirited horse
I hear you in my music,
and I feel you in the wind.
I miss you every day!
—TLC

26

Back into Hell

Elizabeth had nothing of value in her possession. Until that past week, she didn't even have a computer that worked. She did receive an annuity years before, as a result of her accident in Texas. But she cashed it out so many times over the years that there was almost nothing left.

I never discussed this annuity with Elizabeth. It was none of my business, and I had no interest in it. But because the annuity existed, and because it had value years before, when it was awarded to her, she had been advised to draw up a will. Her will named me executor and sole beneficiary of her estate. There was no mention of her father at all anywhere in the document. The will was sent to me by Elizabeth's boyfriend. It was a copy, and in order to process it, I had to find the original, which over the years had been relocated to an unknown attorney's office. This would take an extraordinary amount of time and effort, and I had no strength left … none!

The last thing I felt like doing was scouring the country for the correct document. I was not interested in following through. But, if I did not … I felt like I would be stating that her life was meaningless, and not worth the time and trouble to follow her last request: to clean up her expenses, and let her rest in peace.

If I did proceed, I would be prolonging this horrible grief and incurring a sizable expense in attorney fees, which I wasn't even sure that I could financially absorb. I was filled with sorrow, in shock, and exhausted. I had to get back to work. There were moments when I thought that the pressure was going to kill me, and my second thought was that if it did kill me, it would be a relief.

After careful consideration, against my better judgment, and attempting to make this looming legal ordeal as short and painless as possible for myself, I met with Brian and wife #4. I suggested to them that Brian sign a release, thereby giving me full access to Elizabeth's assets without the will. Then I could just forego the will and follow her instructions on my own. I could clean up her outstanding debt, and pay her expenses.

I expressed to them my depleting strength and stamina, but my enduring desire to get this done.

In return, I proposed that if there was anything left, after all expenses were paid, I would give them half.

They both said, "Oh yes! Thank you! You're so nice to do this!"

I suggested to them that they think about it for a while. I did not want to pay to have a legal document drawn up if they were not going to sign it. They assured me.

So I went ahead and paid to have a legal document drawn up, and Brian and wife #4 never responded. He never signed the document, and he never answered the phone again.

I have only myself to blame for this. Believing that Brian would honor his word was a travesty, and very naive on my part. All Brian had to do was say, "No, I'm not comfortable signing anything" (something that a real person might have done). Apparently, Brian was hoping to get everything, in case there was anything.

This would be the final outrageous encounter with him that I would ever allow. It would be the last time I would be victimized by his lack of civility. I would never again acknowledge Brian's existence, or allow him to affect my life. Now I was determined to proceed on my own, no matter what the cost. And so the legal ordeal began.

It took two years to locate the information that I needed, sending affidavits all over the country to be read, signed and returned. I was charged for every email, every phone call, every stamp, every breath that the attorney took.

There were several times when this process could have been shortened considerably, and thousands of dollars would have been saved, with just a nod from Brian ... but no way was he going to make this easy for me. He hoped right to the end that I would be unsuccessful in this legal endeavor.

I worked a straight sixteen-hour day seven days a week for two years. And every cent that I earned, plus much of my savings, went to the attorney.

I was exhausted and depressed, and still wasn't able to take the time to grieve for my daughter. But there was no doubt that I would see this through no matter what the cost. In my mind, this was the only way that I could honor Elizabeth. It was the last time in my life that I would ever be able to step in and protect her. And, it was the only way that I could live with myself. By the time it was over, most of Elizabeth's assets were swallowed up by legal fees, and I was so tired and confused that I didn't even recognize my life.

Now, for the first time, I had to face Elizabeth's death head on. There were moments when I wished my life was over. It would take another two years to try to recover even a small portion of the funds that were lost.

Three years after her death, I was able to locate a spot where wild horses still roamed; and with permission, I took Elizabeth's remains and scattered them there. Whatever I could salvage from her assets was transferred in her name to the preservation of that land.

During the course of time after Elizabeth died, I found myself filled with rage at the final encounter with my ex-husband. In a feeble vindictive attempt to get his hands on his daughter's estate, or keep me from getting it, he set my life into a tailspin for the second time. Shortly after scattering Elizabeth's ashes, I was diagnosed with advanced debilitating PTSD.

Retirement now seemed nearly impossible. But I had taken such a beating that I was unable to work at a productive pace. I closed down my business at the age of sixty-eight and tried to take a breath. Life was not going to be easy now, but I didn't see any other option.

It's been six years since Elizabeth has died, and the dust has cleared enough for me to attempt to evaluate my own life. I will never be the same person that I was before her death. Still today, when the reality of losing her hits me, as it does, in spurts, I am as stunned as when it first happened. There is no silver lining, no bright side, and no relief from the sorrow.

People often ask one another, "If you could change one event in your life that occurred by choice, what would it be?" The only self-destructive path that I chose in my entire life was my association and marriage to Brian. Every day that I was with him was dark and painful. (That equals seven years of hell, beginning at age sixteen, and that does not include the two confrontational years at the other end.)

After getting away from him, I had initially come to terms with this colossal blunder and made a sincere effort to try to learn something from it.

I had never known dishonesty, deceit, weakness or corruption to such a degree, before Brian. And I have always felt grateful and proud that I found the courage and presence of mind to break away from him, and provide a credible life for myself.

We are all masters of our own destiny. However, it may very well be that the horrendous circumstances of my marriage, to some degree, kept me from ever trusting in another.

I forged ahead in life with a positive attitude, closed the chapter on Brian, and chalked up the time lost to my mixed-up youth and inexperience. In other words, I had no ill will toward him, and hadn't given him another thought.

When Elizabeth died, the interaction that I was forced back into with Brian gave me a clear vision back into hell. *This was astonishing to me!*

His self-serving, blatant disregard for honor and dignity hit me like a Mack® Truck! I guess I had expected that after forty years, he might have grown a little. This disturbing regression back to the past has left me with a residual disgust. And I am not sure that I can wipe the slate clean this time around.

Except for the death of my child, I have always been able to find a positive light on events and people in my life. There is always some lesson to be learned from even the most unpleasant experience.

This, however, is the exception that proves the rule. (Every rule has an exception.) I cannot find one single adjective, thought, conclusion or description in regard to Brian that is not horrific.

27

Danny

As I think back to all the ups and downs of my relationship with my son, I have sadly concluded that I don't have the strength or desire to go through the cycle again and land in the same exact spot that I have landed a hundred times before.

It is said that the definition of insanity is repeating the same behavior, and expecting a different result.

In so many ways, I am indeed proud of him. I do believe that Danny is a successful, productive, adventurous and fun-loving man, with an adequate strength of character. And I give myself credit for all of his positive traits.

What I am saying is that at this point in my life, I don't have the strength to deal with the friction. And I won't put on "kid gloves" to deal with anything!

If I have to strategize this or any relationship, I am clearly just marking time and spinning my wheels in the process.

I have never professed martyrdom, and I would certainly never lay claim to being a martyr now. I don't wish I could be a martyr. I don't even like martyrs!

The bottom line on the issue of Danny is that "It is what it is." And whatever "it" is, I am tired of thinking about it!

28

Grief

People have come into my life, and tried in many different ways to console and give comfort regarding my tragic loss. They all mean well! Some have assured me that God must have loved Elizabeth a little more so she was taken early. While I appreciate all the sensitivity and effort of everyone who tried to bring some relief, I have to tell you … that there is no relief. And I really never bought the "God took her early" scenario. Even if that were true, it wouldn't help. Or I should say, it wouldn't help me!

So for all who are grieving, a word of sincere compassion. In the attempt to be of some help, I am sharing the conclusions that I have come to as a result of my own experience:

Grief is excruciating, unbearable, unrelenting, never ending, and hopeless.

It is the equivalent of sitting in a small boat in the hot sun, bobbing up and down, in the middle of the sea, with no oars, no wind, and no land in sight. You're just there listening to the sound of nothing. The sun is hot, and the movement of the boat conjures up a feeling that borders on nausea, while you attempt with all your might, to make sense of anything.

There is no way to ease the pain and confusion. The harder you try, the worse it becomes. There is nothing you can do except feel it. Feel all of it deeply!

There are numerous large terrifying waves that simply take you. You cannot escape them. You cannot escape any of it.

Fate has dealt you a blow that has more gravity than you have ever felt before. This is now part of your life. Learning to live with it is your only hope!

Every day you must summon the strength ... not to fight it, but to accept it.

This will never get better, but it might get different.

Once you have done all that you can do to come to terms, not with the loss, but with the new path that has been thrust upon you, you must embrace the spirit of moving forward.

Do not diminish the value of your own life by remaining caught up in missing the value of your lost loved one's.

I am not suggesting that you try to forget about your loss. I am simply saying that ... although death affects many lives, it should only take one!

29

Elizabeth

Now that years have passed since the tragedy of Elizabeth's death, I am able to focus mostly on the extraordinary gift of her last visit, and the flawless moment-to-moment interaction that we shared together during that visit, from beginning to end.

I am able to thank God for that profound and meaningful sojourn.

I am grateful for the deep personal connections that we made.

I am grateful for the uncontrollable laughter.

I am grateful that I recognized Elizabeth's newly acquired confidence, maturity, and wisdom.

I am grateful that I told her that she was so beautiful.

I am grateful that she loved me.

And, I am so grateful that she was happy!

30

The Journey

Having rounded the corner of seventy-one last year, I am focusing on getting the most life out of my remaining years. Except for the financial challenge, retirement has been a blessing.

My most meaningful achievements have been realized in this present time period of my life. After thirty years of round-the-clock working, I have finally found time to develop and nurture previous interests.

I am an avid pianist, and have written several musical compositions.

I hike often with my dogs.

I have found endless ways to stretch food in a most healthy manner. And I have developed several wonderful recipes. I bake often.

I am pleased to say that my daily routine can finally be classified in the "early to bed, early to rise" category.

I am beyond grateful to have made the personal choices that brought me to this house thirty-three years ago, and still feel privileged every time I look out a window.

My friendships have blossomed far beyond what words could ever express. I am the luckiest person in the world to have such good people in my life—always supportive … never judging … always caring. My friends are, and have been, an abundance of riches.

If I could describe myself in a definitive manor, with pride, I would say:

I am not a game player. I say what I mean, and I do what I say, without exception!

I am credible and I am honorable.

There are no gray areas in my life. Things are black or they are white.

I miss my parents!

I think of my father often.

And I would love to have Sicilian Pizza for lunch with my mother, and then watch her eat a Charlotte Russe for dessert!

> *When peace like a river attendeth my way,*
> *when sorrows like sea billows roll;*
> *whatever my lot, thou has taught me to say,*
> *"It is well, it is well with my soul."*
> —Horatio G. Spafford

Made in the USA
Columbia, SC
25 September 2018